Printing and Embroidery

Window panel. 'Pellagoniums' by Christine Garwood
photograph by John Hunnex

The background retains subtle colourings whilst the foreground is contrastingly bright. The whole panel was embroidered on an Irish machine, and the fabric attached to the frame by hand. The plants were padded with terylene wadding, and the applied strips of fabric were worked over using various coloured threads of embroidery cotton to match the printed fabric used. The gradation of colour and stitchery was achieved by various spool tensions and close, concentrated stitchery round the padded plants, becoming freer and larger towards the top, and covering most of the panel

Mary Newland
Carol Walklin

Printing and Embroidery

Photography by
Colin Walklin

BT Batsford Ltd London

© *Mary Newland*
and Carol Walklin 1977
First published 1977
ISBN 0 7134 0136 2

Filmset by
Servis Filmsetting Ltd, Manchester
Printed in Great Britain by
The Anchor Press, Tiptree, Essex
for the publishers
B.T. Batsford Ltd
4 Fitzhardinge Street
London W1H 0AH

Contents

Introduction 6

Approaches 10

The natural world 14

The man-made world 34

Using photography 44

People 54

Graphics 64

Collections 70

Looking forward 82

Further reading 85

Suppliers 86

Acknowledgment 88

Index 89

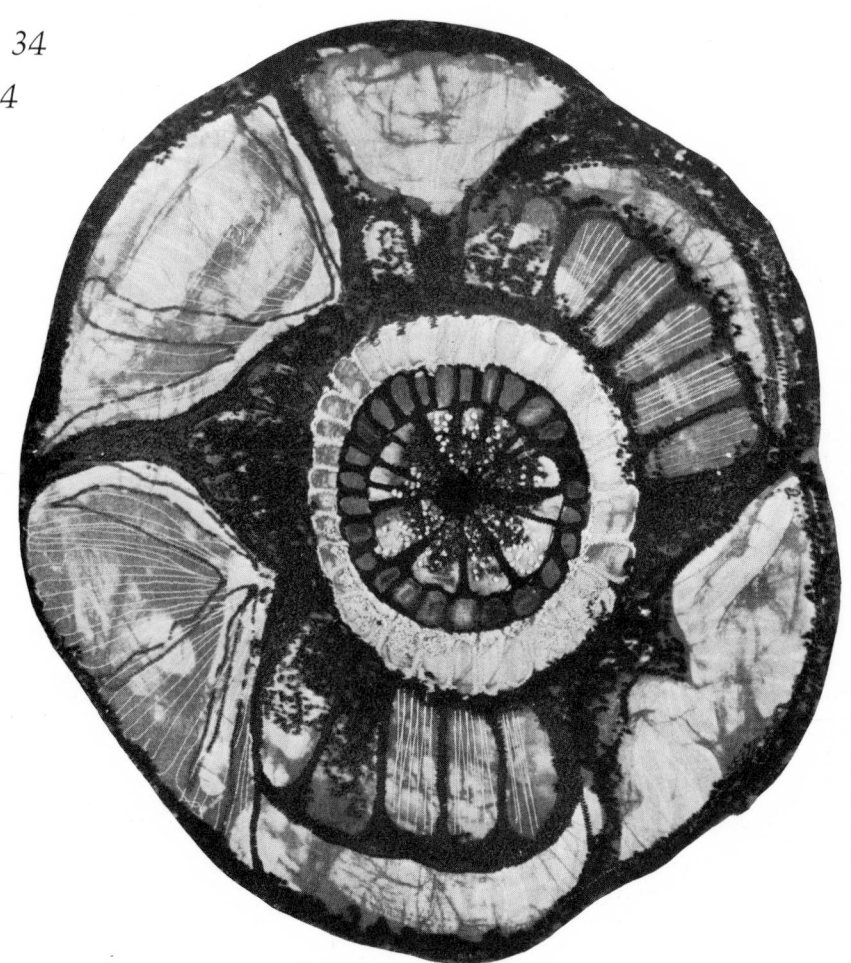

Introduction

Up to the nineteen-sixties images on fabric tended to make use of the craft of embroidery and pure stitchery. These traditional methods were often imitative of painting, creating a 'picture', as in the Bradford carpet (illustrated left). More self-conscious stitchery, where the actual individual stitches impose themselves on the design, is characteristic of work of the nineteen-fifties.

Attitudes have altered, technology progressed. It is now possible for the artist to use many and varied techniques with which to express ideas, and to make individual visual statements. It is acceptable to combine several differing techniques, manipulating skills, and using a much wider visual vocabulary. Mixed media can be synonymous with muddle, but this is seen less often now that colleges of education and schools of art are encouraging the sensitive use of this creative, fine-art approach to embroidery.

The 'embroiderer' *per se* was once a member of a minority group, having a distinct craft emphasis, which has now been joined by artists and designers, so bringing together the skills of craftsmanship and intellect. This amalgamation has made greater demands on the designer. So-called 'fine art' can often be a self-centred occupation, but to create images on fabric successfully there has to be a mastery of many skills. The disciplines of drawing and analysis, colour theories, uses of textures, require great skill and sensitivity in their combina-

Detail of the Bradford Table Carpet, *English, late sixteenth century. Linen canvas embroidered with silks in tent stitch*
Victoria and Albert Museum, London

tion and balance. Altogether, embroidery has become a far more demanding and intellectual art form.

The time factor, as well as advancing technology, has played a part in this change. Traditional hand embroidery needs *time*. Historically, embroidery was once a time-filler as well as a beautiful and practical craft. Speedier techniques such as printing, collage, direct drawing and painting onto fabric, and the newer sewing machines with their built-in stitch-changes and tensions, have the qualities of spontaneity, a characteristic which seems more appropriate for the tempo of our present society and its claims. These qualities also serve to enrich the final statement of the artist and designer.

Often artists have worked at length on a personal theme, a single idea or obsession, seeking for the right interpretation and methods, using the fabric as their 'canvas'. Sometimes these efforts emerge as pictorial, visual comments on faces or places. Sometimes they are giving expression to a deeply felt emotion or a totally abstract concept.

The illustrations in this book have been taken from the work of both established designers and students. They have been selected to underline the personal approach and progressions of the artist, from the initial impetus through to the near-final or final statement. We do not seek to direct but to encourage and stimulate. Not all finished products are shown but many developments are given in the hope that these will help the reader to experiment and explore with sensitivity, his or her personal approach to creating *images on fabric*.

Beckenham, Kent 1977   MN and CW

Al fuoco! Al fuoco! *(Fire! Fire!) by Enrico Baj 1963–64*
Mexican. *Green and red painted figure with metal collage on furnishing fabric background*
The Tate Gallery, London. Presented by Avvocato Paride Accenti 1973

Approaches

We cannot work from 'nothing', there has to be an initial impetus. This impetus can be initiated by an abstract idea or by actual visual stimuli.

We *can* work from anything, providing we know how to 'see'. The training of the seeing eye is essential to all artists and designers. Opportunities are everywhere – no two people see alike, but learning to see selectively, is a continuing discipline, it does not just 'happen' but comes with much practice and perseverence. One learns to select and simplify, working gradually towards the final statement; retaining and discarding, choosing the appropriate media with which to work.

Recognition of the basic elements of design helps the beginner. Line, shape, colour, texture, pattern, play their part in the nature of things and ideas. Awareness of them and the sensitive use of them gives structure to the work.

As to subjects, something more than just 'delight' is needed. To convert this delight (or antipathy), into a visual statement that can communicate the designers' feelings, they must be able to bring together image and skill.

Work illustrating some of these themes are grouped here under the headings The Natural World; The Man-made World; People; Photography; Graphics and Collections. Each section has a short preamble but this is a visual book with the pictures making their own main points, the words serving only to reinforce these points or to describe a technique.

The natural world

The man-made world

Using photography

People

Graphics

Collections

The natural world

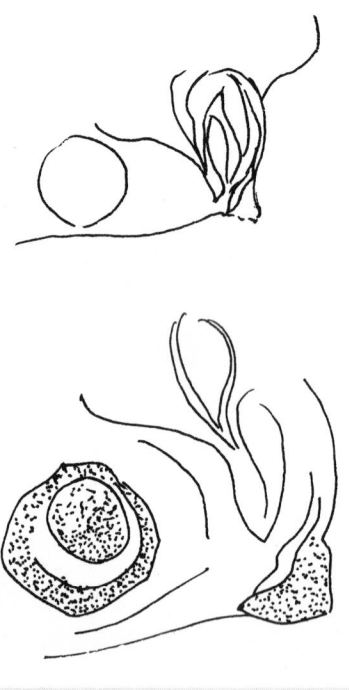

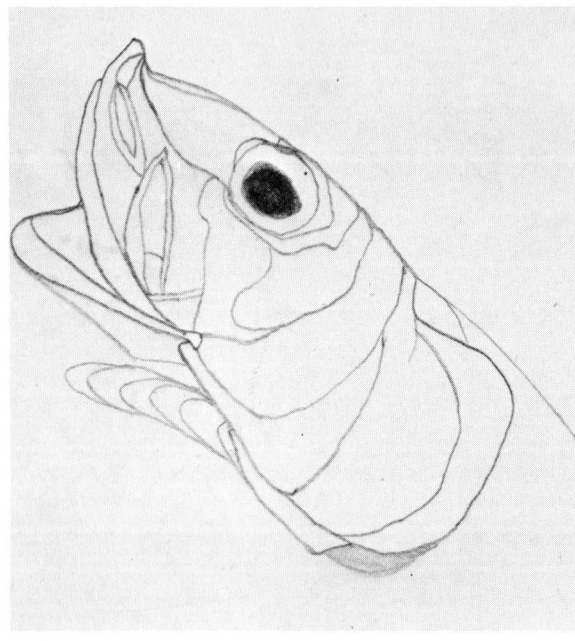

The natural world offers the designer endless opportunities for creative ideas. Even in an urban environment the natural world can be found in a crack in a pavement filled with growing plant forms, city birds, trees in a park. Nature need not be 'pretty' to be visually stimulating. Weeds and mould have qualities as exciting as magnolia blossom or reflections in a stream.

The five basic elements of design are readily found in the world of nature, sometimes to an overwhelming degree. It is often necessary to consider which quality is the most characteristic, which the most dominant.

Some subjects are linear in feeling, others depend on colour for their impact, but most combine more than one element. It is the designers' task to express and state the special qualities as best they can. They should not try to slavishly imitate Nature or improve on it, rather they should make a strong, visual, *personal* statement which can be readily understood by others.

The richness of the natural world is so great that it helps to divide it for study into those things seen *closely* and those seen from *afar*; that is to say, the magnified detail of a daisy-head to a distant landscape. Both very different in scale but each requiring the same concentration of selection and rejection.

Abstracting designs from close observation of fish head
Above left   *Fine pen by Kathy Locke*
Left   *Pencil by Marion Woods*

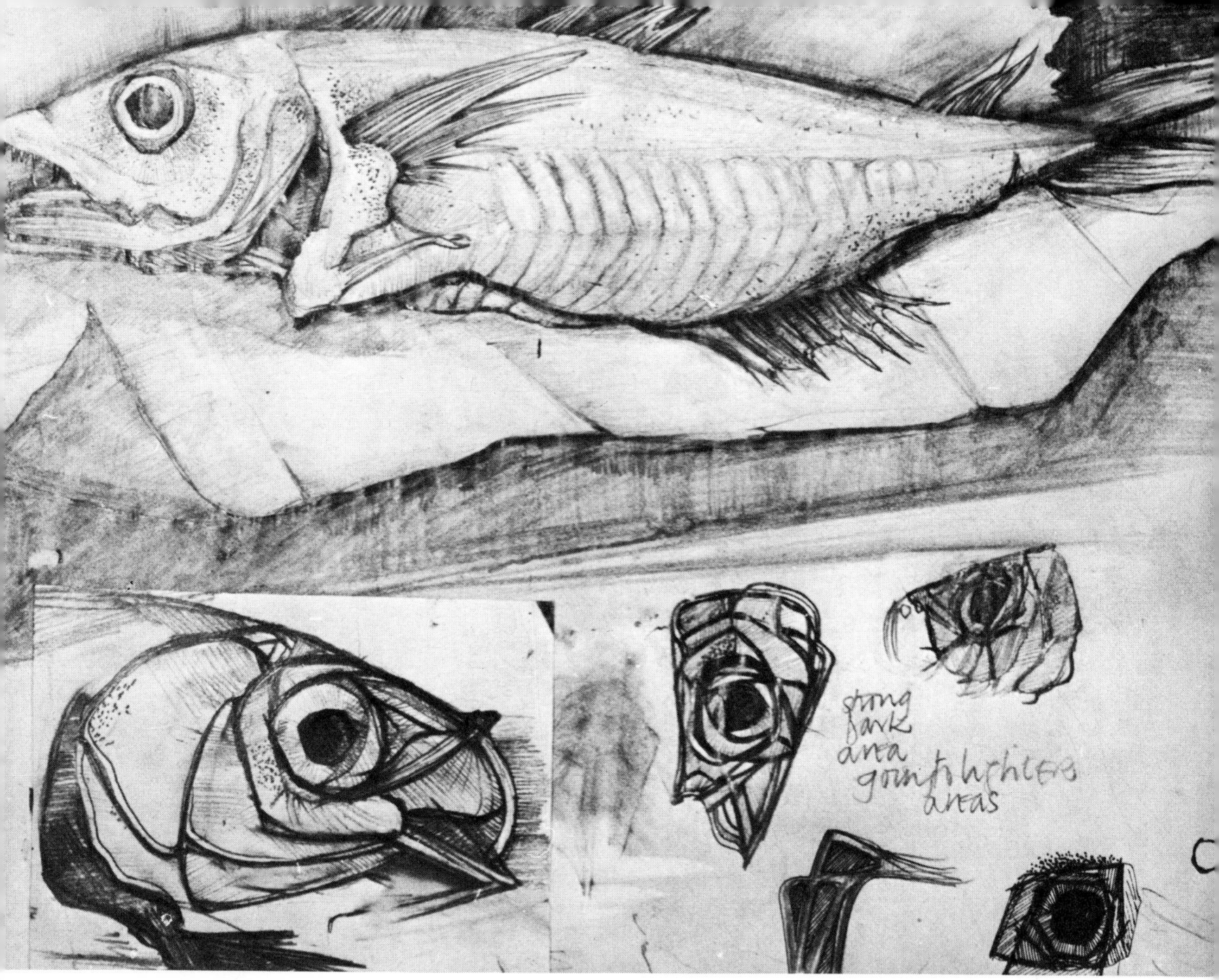

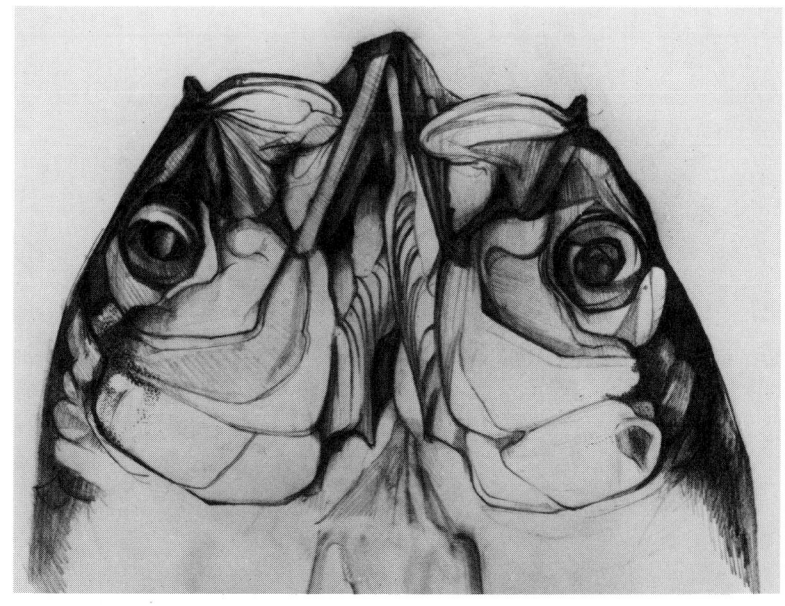

Fish *Close observations of fish, starting with a carefully controlled study of the whole fish, and then looking for structure of parts, isolating them, and getting closer and closer with the aid of a magnifying glass. A strong linear approach has been used but also heavy areas have been built up to give strength and weight. Pencil by Mary Newland*

A hollyhock flowerhead and its seed pod each offer differing qualities for interpretation. Close study of the structure and the form provide the designer with ideas both for three-dimensional work and experimental work in textiles
Right   *The screenprinted image is white on white organdie with hand and machine stitchery also in white*

Right *Batik print with additional drawing in oil bound pastels and some hand and machine embroidery*

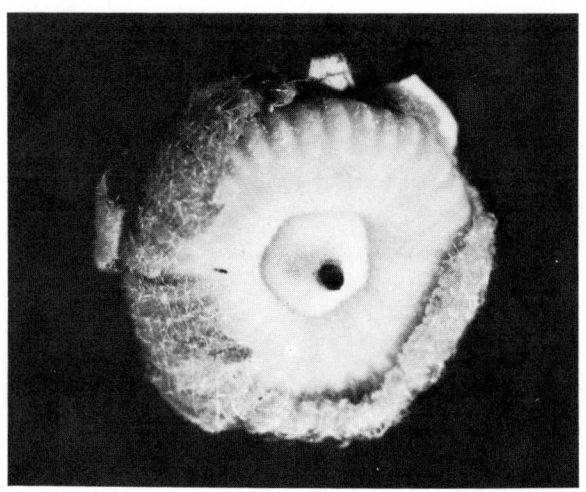

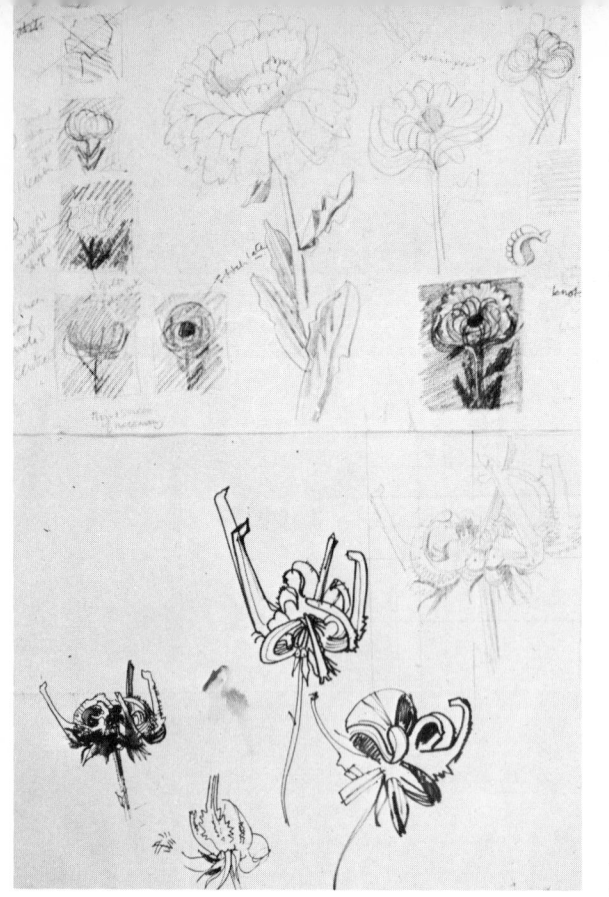

Design based on a marigold flowerhead with its dead counterpart. The two have been brought together to create a double image of 'dead and alive'. One series of studies shows the careful planning of the colour sequences in batik for the alive version, the other shows drawings of the seed-head

Right *The final screenprinted image of the dead seedhead using a photographic stencil*

Detail *This illustrates the advantages of* direct drawing *on to the linen fabric. A felt tip was used to reinforce the rhythms of some of the batik areas and some accidental shapes are continued and elaborated in a decorative manner. The flower centre is given a textural 'lift' and added richness by using silk threads and closely spaced french knots*

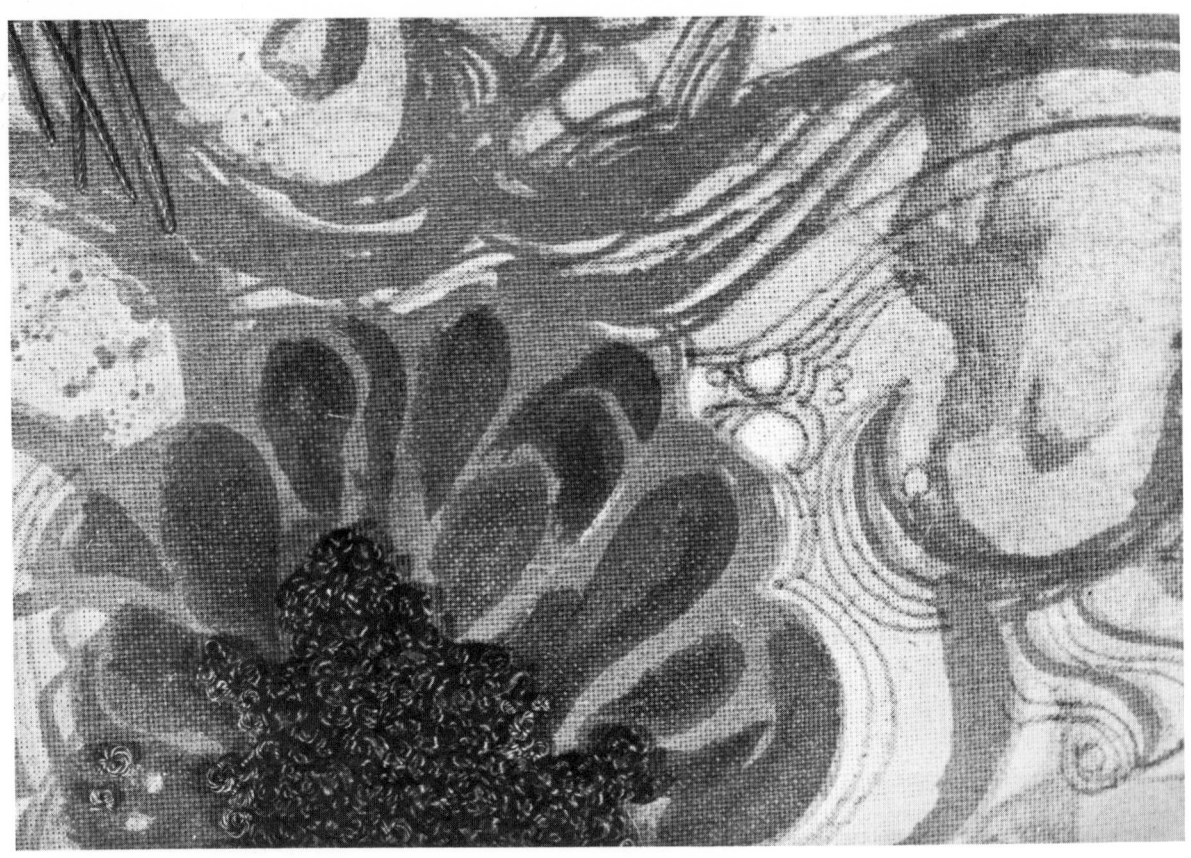

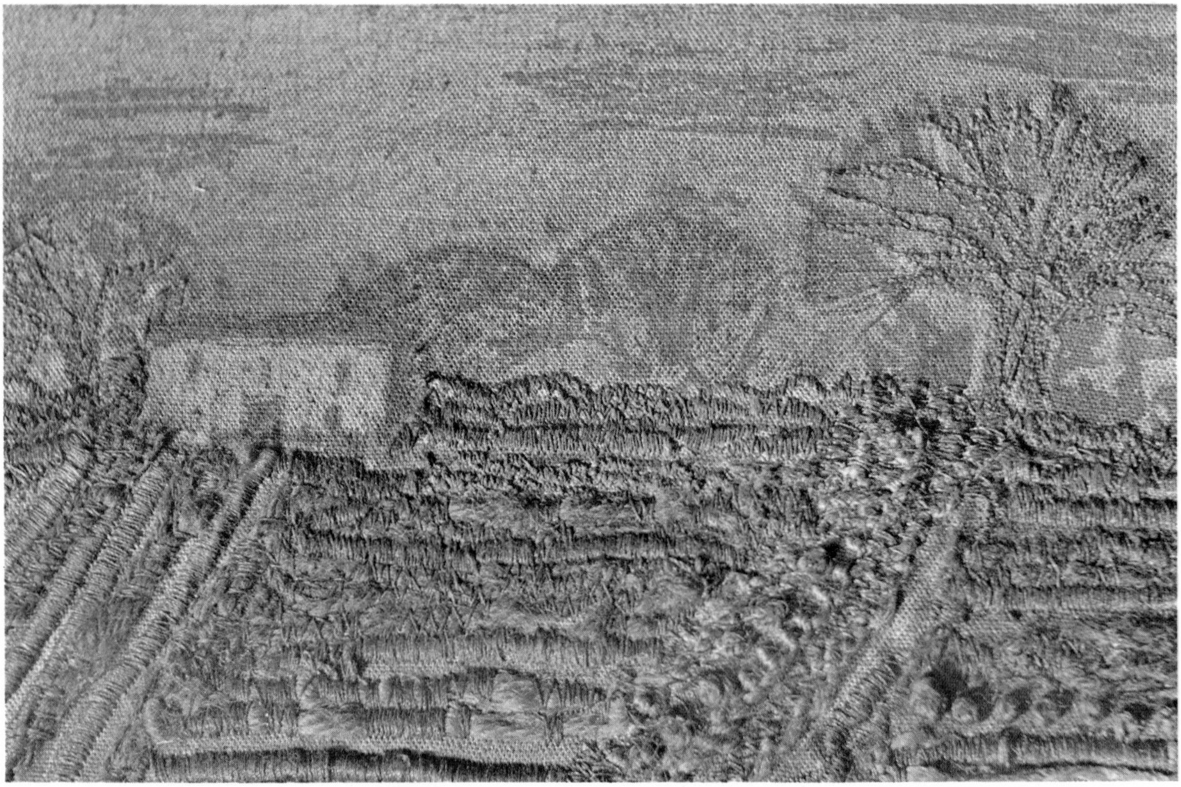

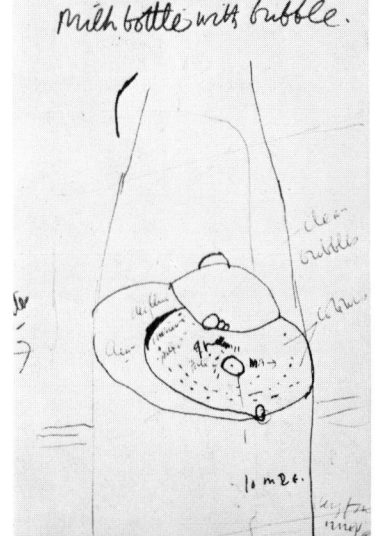

milk bottle with bubble.

The fragile, trapped soap-bubble in the milk bottle, catches the sun which creates ephemeral but brilliant rings of purples and greens, contrasting with the colder surfaces of glass and stainless steel
Foot of page   Threads have been laid on to a fabric background, collaged with PVA adhesive. The superimposed 'bubble' is made from satin, stretched over an oval card cutout with some padding   Carol Walklin

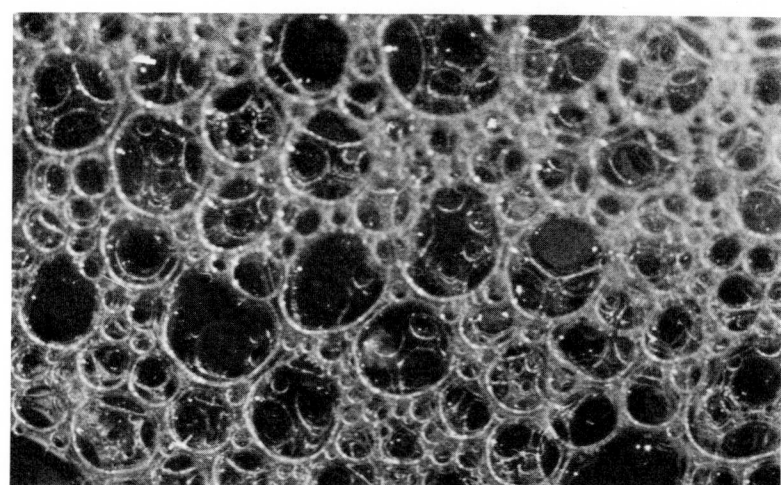

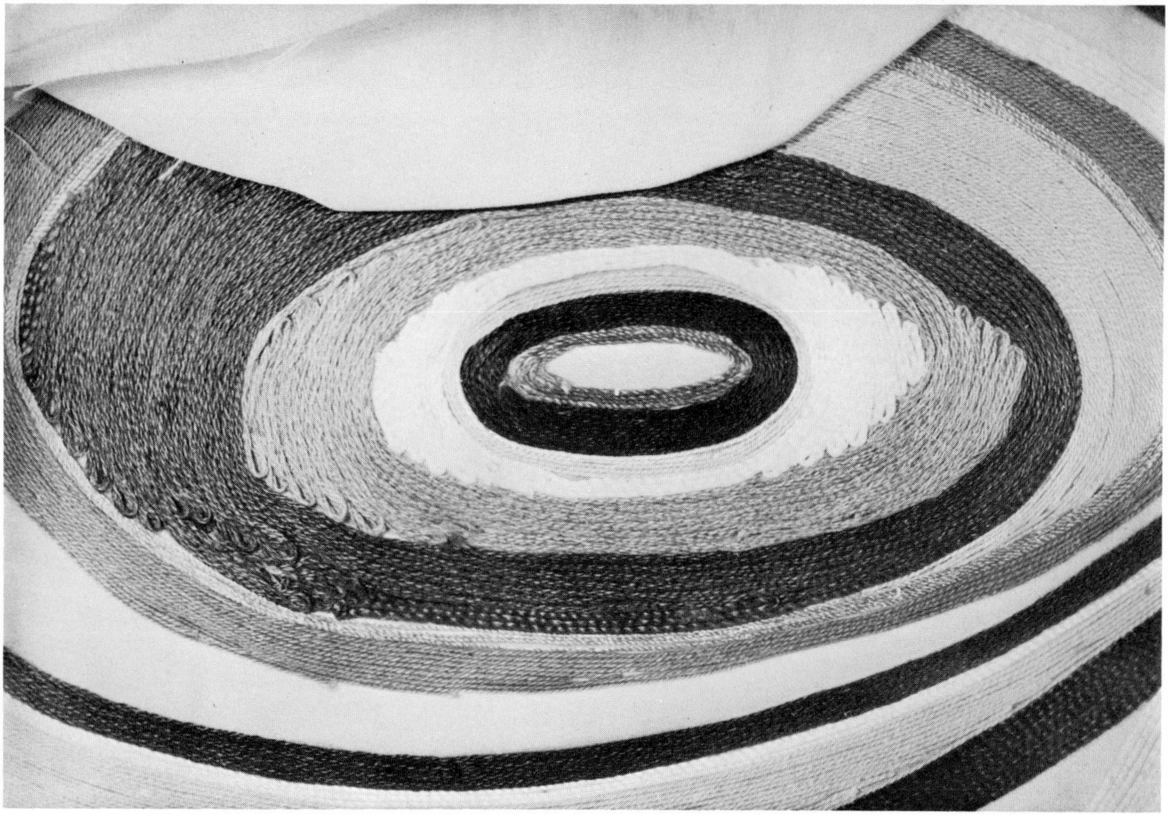

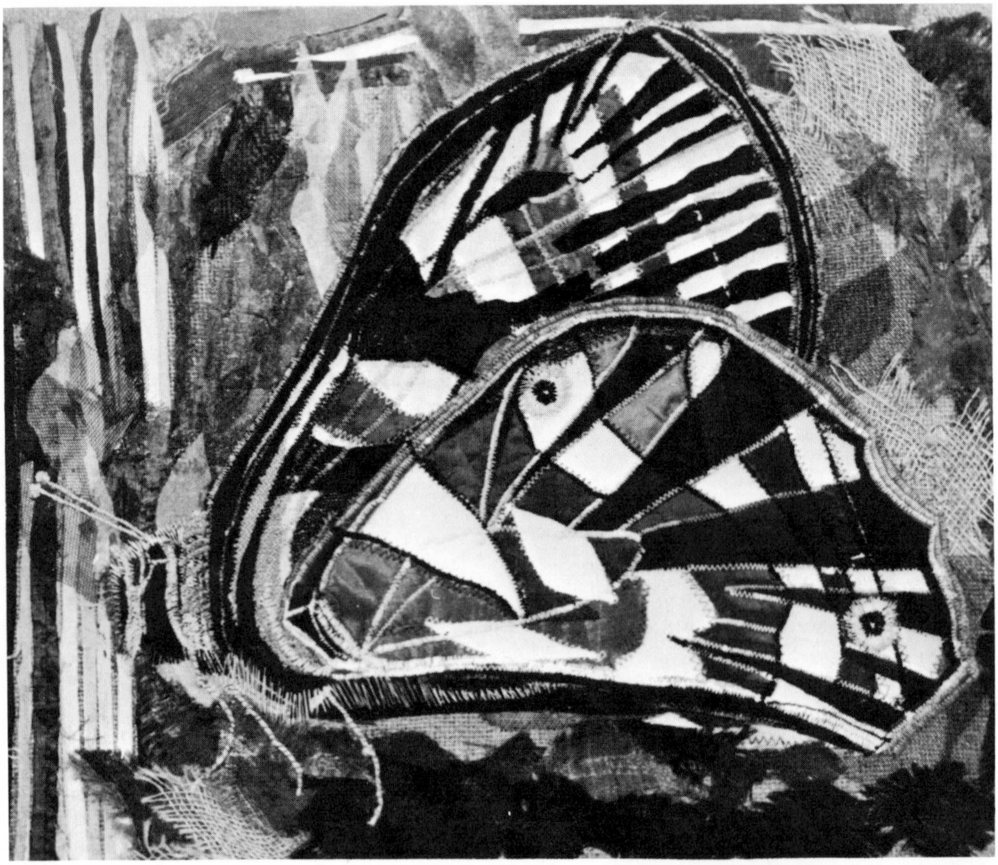

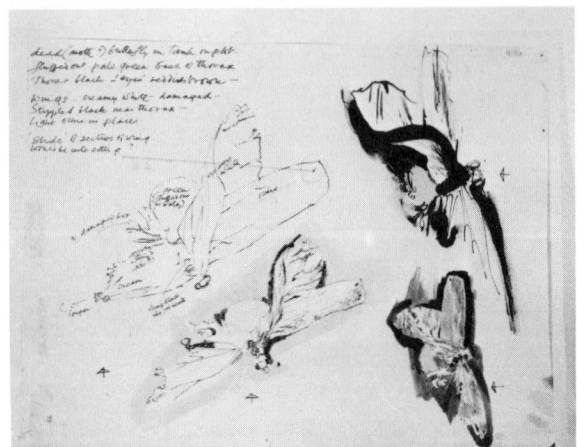

Butterfly, *camouflaged on its collaged background, with screenprinted areas, worked over with hand and machine embroidery by Joy Stringer*

Dead Moth, *based on observation, using applied fabrics and hand stitchery on black hessian by Carol Walklin*

Studies of fungus forms
Fungus form, screenprinted with a
paper stencil on to sailcloth using one
colour. Line and form was reinforced
by machine quilting in self colour
Virginia Harman
Drawing by Carol Walklin

23

Barbara Siedlecka

These pages show an artist at work: drawing from a boat, having to work quickly putting down immediate reactions. The time factor helping the artist to select Preoccupation with linear perspective, textural qualities, the dried stiff grasses and reeds, the dykes, water and reflections, the changing colours of the new, bright grass, details of birds, all make a fascinating microcosm of the Norfolk Broads. See colour plate facing page 20

These three progressions show drawings from the first representational observations to the more selective, abstracted forms

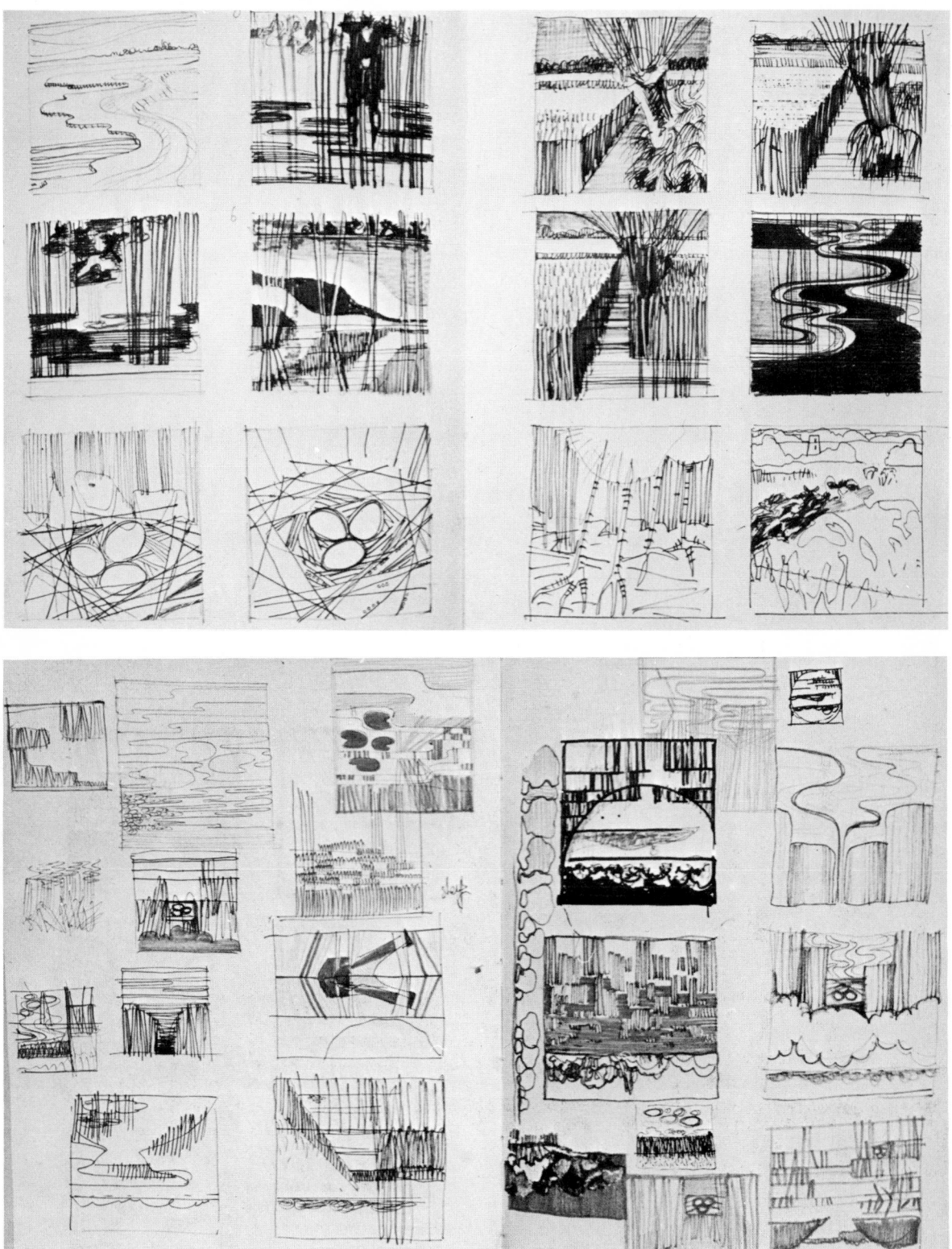

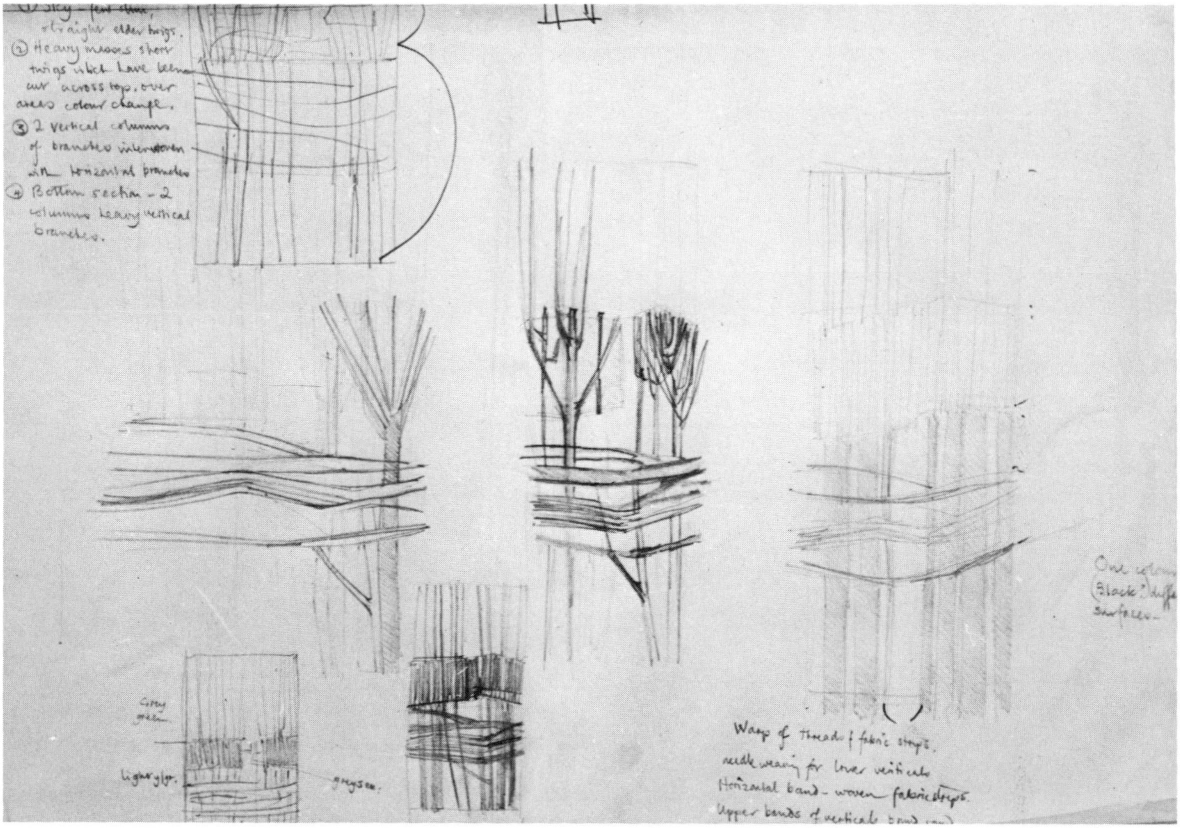

The hedge has become a grid, a network of lines, through which the fields appear as geometric patches of colour. The structure of the hedge shows up well through the early spring twigs

Pulled threadwork and needleweaving interpretation of hedge studies   Pamela Whatmore

27

Here, studies of natural forms in a water garden provide interesting contrasts of shapes – cast shadows, densities, the light playing through the more transparent forms in addition to the light seen through the tunnel of foliage   Jan Beaney

 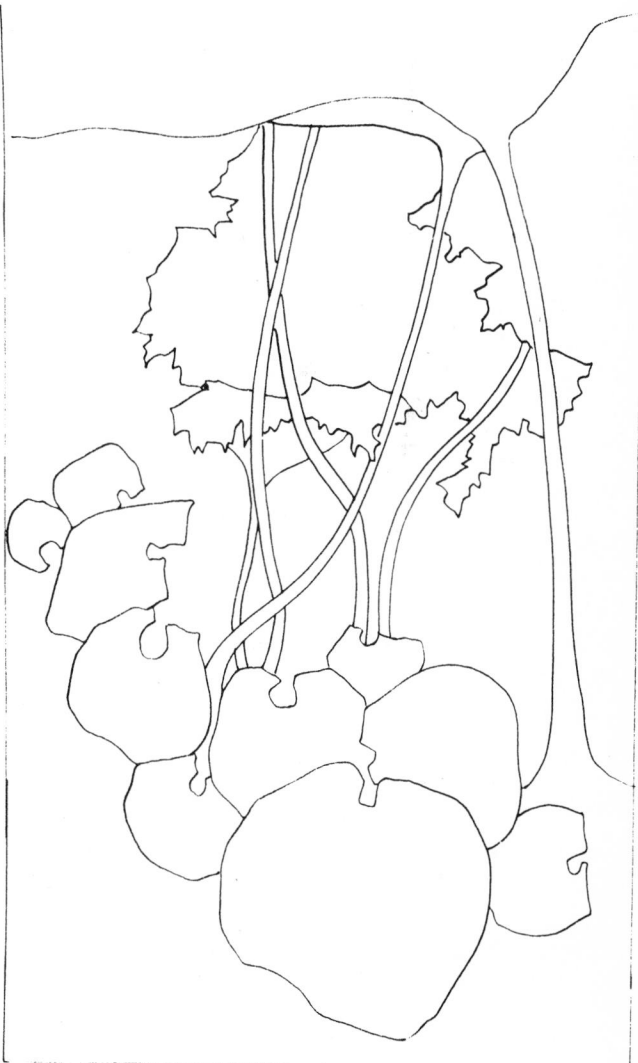

The rigid lines of the fencing breaks up a familiar scene into smaller sections without losing the unity of the whole landscape
The six sections were worked separately and then linked with the wooden fence structure
The landscape has applied fabrics, overlapping organdies, suggesting distance ; thin card wrapped around with threads for buildings ; and tree and hedge forms in ruched velvets
The field was hand-painted with printing dyes and highlighted with threads   Pamela Whatmore

30

Golf Course   *A darker green screenprint, using a photographic stencil, printed on a lighter green hessian background with machine stitching. (Moss stitch and tufting.) The finished image included padding and some additional felt tip drawing (unfinished)*   Mary Newland

Allotment *(Left)* *Screenprinted image using photographic stencil on calico, with some hand painting, also hand and machine embroidery and collaged beansticks. Rapidograph drawn detail for distance*
Mary Newland

Welsh Valley *Freely interpreted and mainly collaged landscape on hessian, with padded hills, overlaid nets, some simple hand and machine stitchery by Sarah Walklin*

The man-made world

Preliminary work showing spiralled, collaged Lurex threads on the crushed can which has been made from a cardboard cutout with felt–tip drawing. The 'tag' is also a cutout. The can becomes 'extraordinary' and is elevated to the richness of its brocade background   Carol Walklin

At first, the man–made world may seem less appealing than that of the natural, but it has much to offer too. The apparently ordinary can become *extra-ordinary* seen with a fresh and discerning eye. It certainly can have equal impact and it avoids the sometimes hackneyed or sentimentalised approaches that can gather around the more conventional themes provided by nature.

The visual qualities are not so immediately obvious in the man–made world and it takes some measure of courage to present certain kinds of material with sensitivity and conviction. 'Pop' art has been accepted and, by its acceptance, widens the scope for the designer working in fabric and thread.

Machinery, buildings, food, packaging, refuse, these are some of the areas that have proved stimulating to the designer willing to attempt a 'sea change', although in fact many of such objects have their own beauty without the help of another medium.

Each generation brings its own new vision to art and design. Although we still appreciate and utilise the natural world with gratitude, the statements made from looking perceptively and sensitively at our own, man–made world, can make a valuable contribution, reflecting our society, making comments even if not always favourable ones.

The five elements are less evident, requiring designers to make even greater efforts to select and emphasise qualities of line or structure, colour or tone, to elevate the choice of subject.

Collage interpretation of crushed can

34

Buildings, treeforms, both structures of great strength, but the one impenetrable, the other more like windows, revealing sometimes, sometimes merging. Finnish scenes have stimulated the artist to explore the correlation of man-made and natural structure   *Barbara Siedlecka*

Scrapyard *From well observed studies this is mainly collage on fabric, over screenprinting (paper stencil), with painting and drawing, also hand and machine stitchery Phil Banister*

Park Bench *A screenprint (paper stencil) repeat in three tones of brown, with some hand stitchery and collaged PVC. Lines added by printing with a card edge dipped in paint Anita Jeapes*

Skylines and scaffolding are the points of departure for the panel which uses simple printing techniques, with 'junk' blocks; matchbox ends, card edges, offcuts of wood etc; with some hand and machine stitching. Additional drawing with oil-bound pastels and felt tip pens   Joan Egan

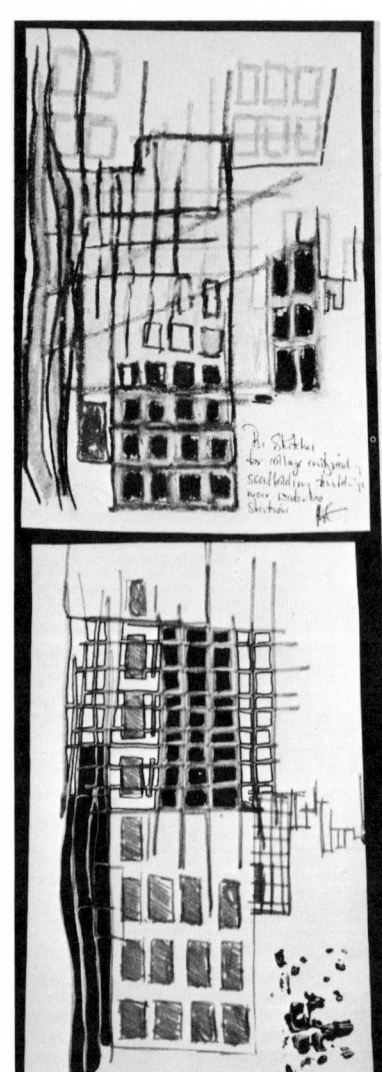

Country Cottage   *This image was made on natural coloured fabric with machine embroidery. Patches of black and grey Vilene were stuck down for brick textures and windows. Foreground with plant forms is in machine embroidery which also picks out mortar and brick patterns. The whole was worked from a black and white photograph   Josette Kooraram*

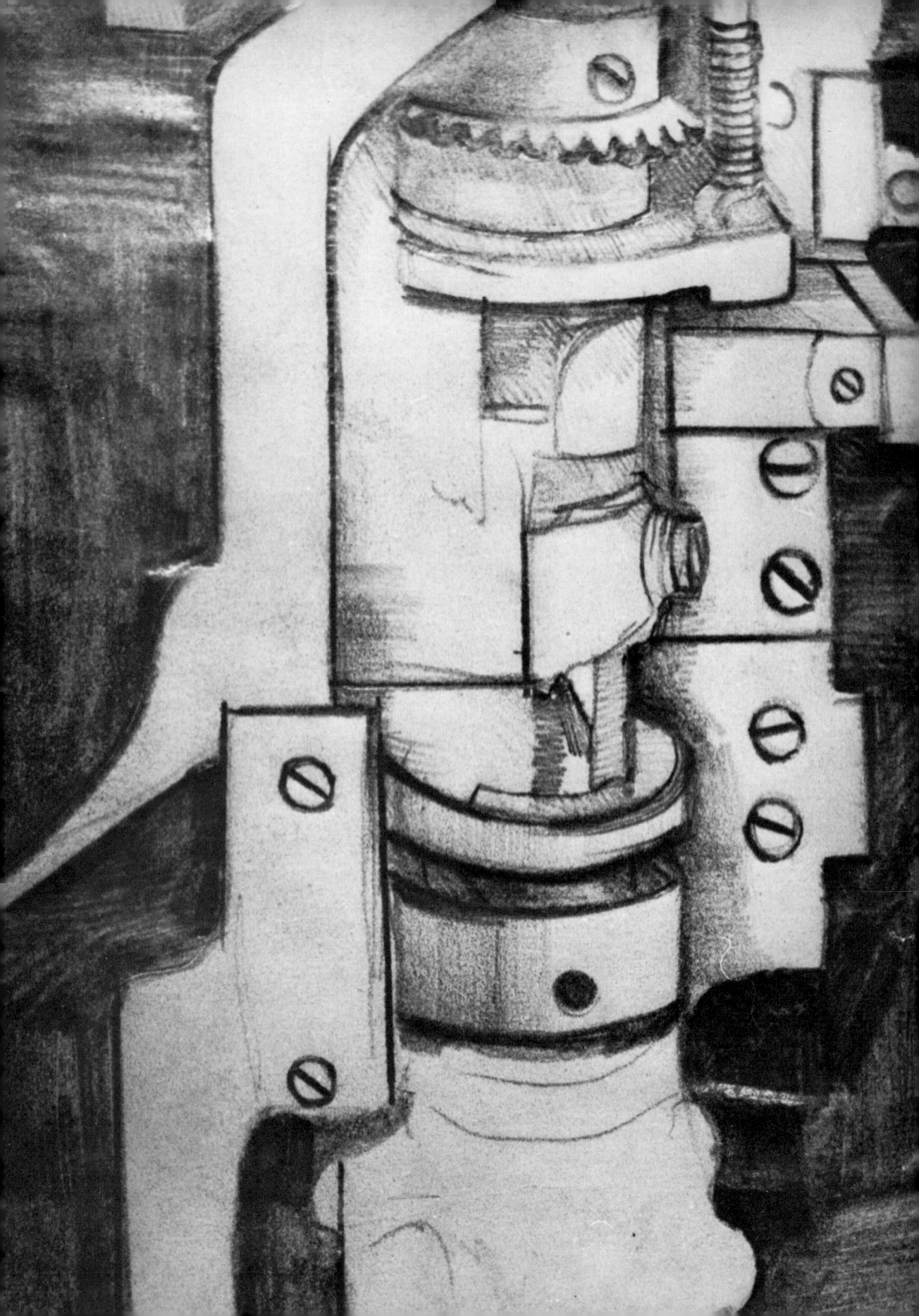

Preparatory work for a series of panels based on studies of a printing press. To be carried out as a screenprinting (photographic stencil) with added lines of thread to lift the surface   Mary Newland

printed bag
embroidered sweets.
on edge of printed
line to suggest → three dimensional sweet
fallen from bag.

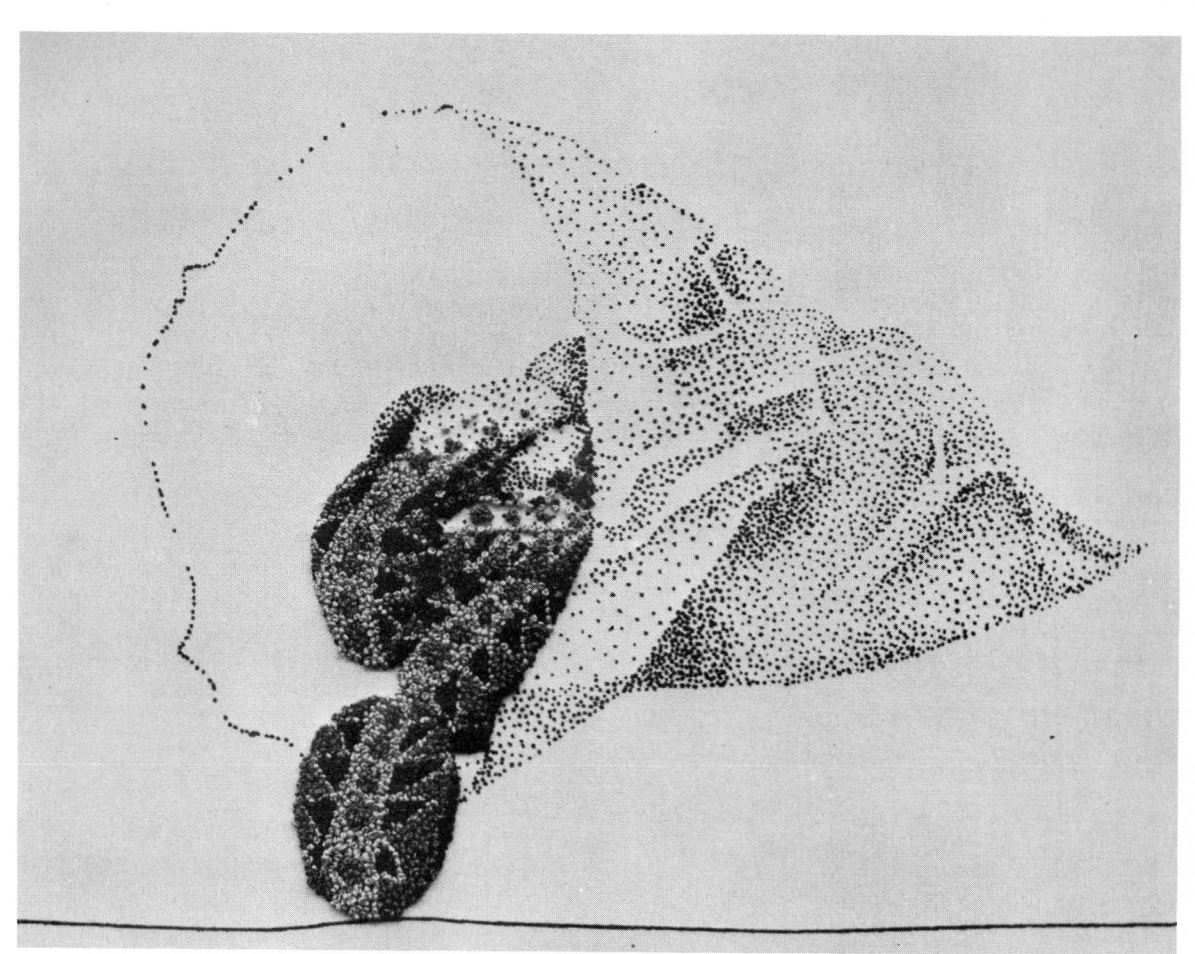

Screenprinted (photographic stencil) sweet bag with sweets enriched with knots as texture and brilliant colour. Fallen single 'sweet' is mounted onto the background fabric to appear almost three-dimensional
Margaret Garner

This panel attempts to show the contrasting small scale and jewel-like patterned qualities of the sweets and the uncertainty of the precarious balance on a horizontal line depicting an 'edge'. The fallen sweet is intentionally placed on a large, empty area to give greater impact

Using photography

Photography falls into two main categories: firstly, using the work of others, secondly using the camera ourselves, that is, being our own photographer.

Using the work of others we obviously get a second-hand reaction, but we may never be able to see that face, visit that place, or catch that fleeting moment. Still, the initial stimulus has been commissioned or felt by another. However, there are advantages. Good composition is often ready-made or we can re-select with our own 'cuts' or frames. Tonal effects in black and white photography can provide excellent reference. There are technical devices too, probably beyond our skill; that of conscious distortion, 'fish eye' lens, stroboscopic movements, actions that the mere human eye cannot register.

The selective processes are still needed, for to be just 'photographic' is not creative. But maybe there are some unusual colours found by the cameraman, an incredible viewpoint and so on, nevertheless, unless we have recourse to the original source of the picture we can be left high and dry if adhering too closely to the reproduction, which can be frustrating.

Using a camera ourselves provides selection from the very start and, with luck, reliable reference, an added dimension to our source and sketchbooks. Often things are impermanent and we need to catch the moment or condition – shadows pass and objects deteriorate.

We can consciously use the camera when the idea is already in the evolving process, but it is also useful for building up a visual store of material. This can be valuable as reference which may well suggest ideas for designs some time later. Sketches and photographs can often evoke a strong memory, as well as reinforce actual information about a place or incident. As our technical skill improves, our opportunities widen, and we will find that our scrapbooks, source books and our own photographs will be of great use.

Opposite   *Marigold by Carol Walklin*
See also pages 18–20

Photograph by Michael J Pickering

often it is the first plant to grow after a fire

Willowherb or fireweed inspired these designs. The lettering was taken from a paragraph in a BBC Schools educational publication on Wild Flowers in England which was reinforced with actual observations with additional information and ideas from studies of individual plant forms

Below *With photographic stencils, three bands of colour were screenprinted. The lettering, gorsebush drawing and 'blots' of badly burned grass were then overprinted in black using a photographic stencil. The suggestion, of the willowherb foliage was made in the same way. The briar is printed from a flocked linoblock*
Above right *Additional painting with fabric dyes and drawing with oilbound pastels*
Lower right *Applied nets on the flowerheads with some knots; added painting on the briar and thorns with poster colours and powder paint; simple line stitches in differing kinds of threads for grass textures*

often it is the first plant to grow after a fire

often it is the first plant to grow after a fire

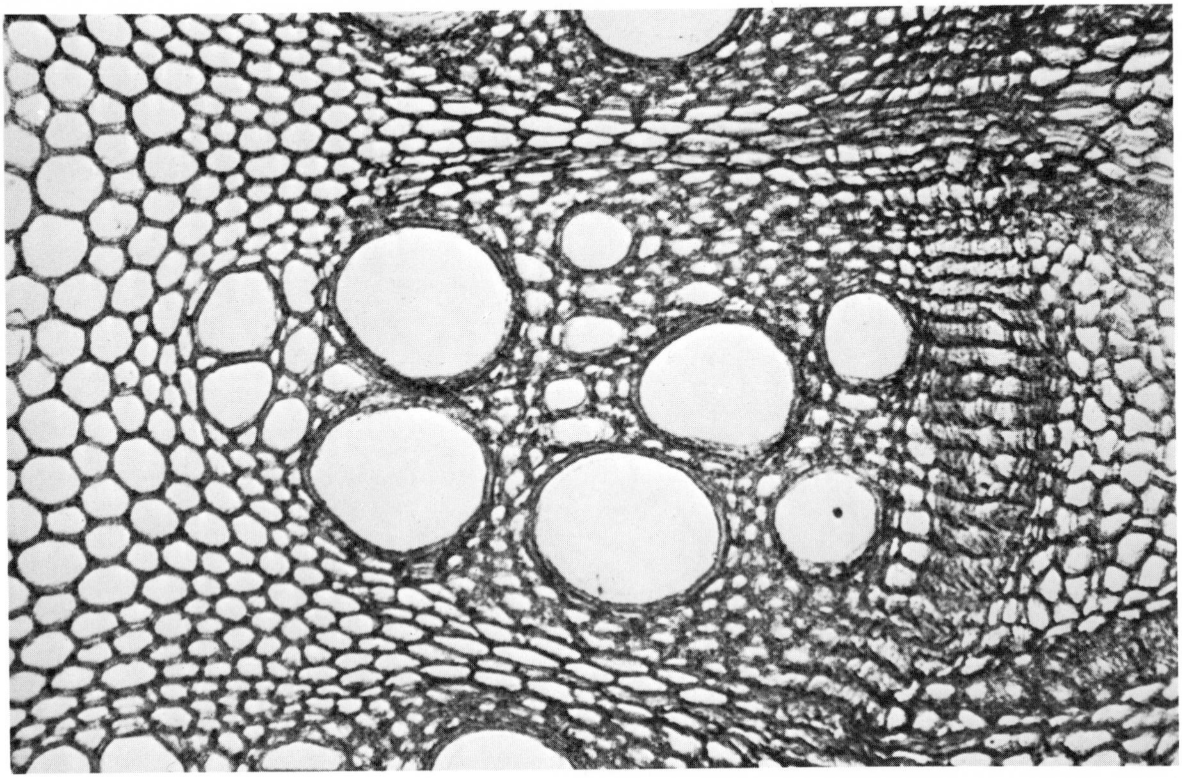

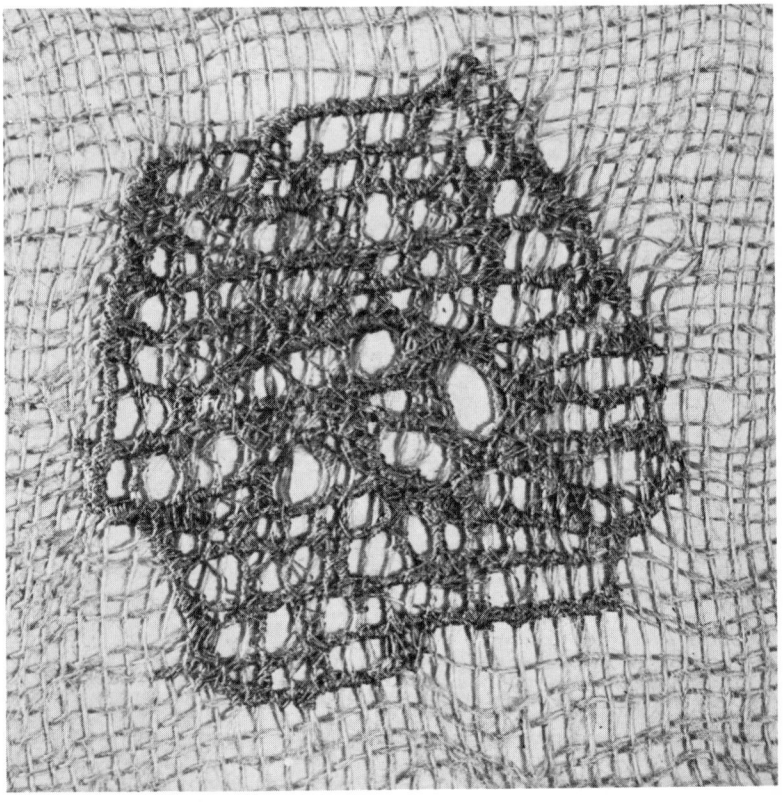

Cell structure picture from a biology book, interpreted into a design on open scrim, with free machine embroidery   Rita Mathewson

Screenprinted landscape on beige corduroy, inspired by a colour supplement picture. Fabric has been applied with a simple domestic machinery which has been used also to 'draw' and texture the landscape. (A first use of this technique)
Diane Davidson

Couching, paddling, needle-weaving, drawn thread-work, the design taken from a reproduction of a Van Gogh painting   Sheila Armstrong

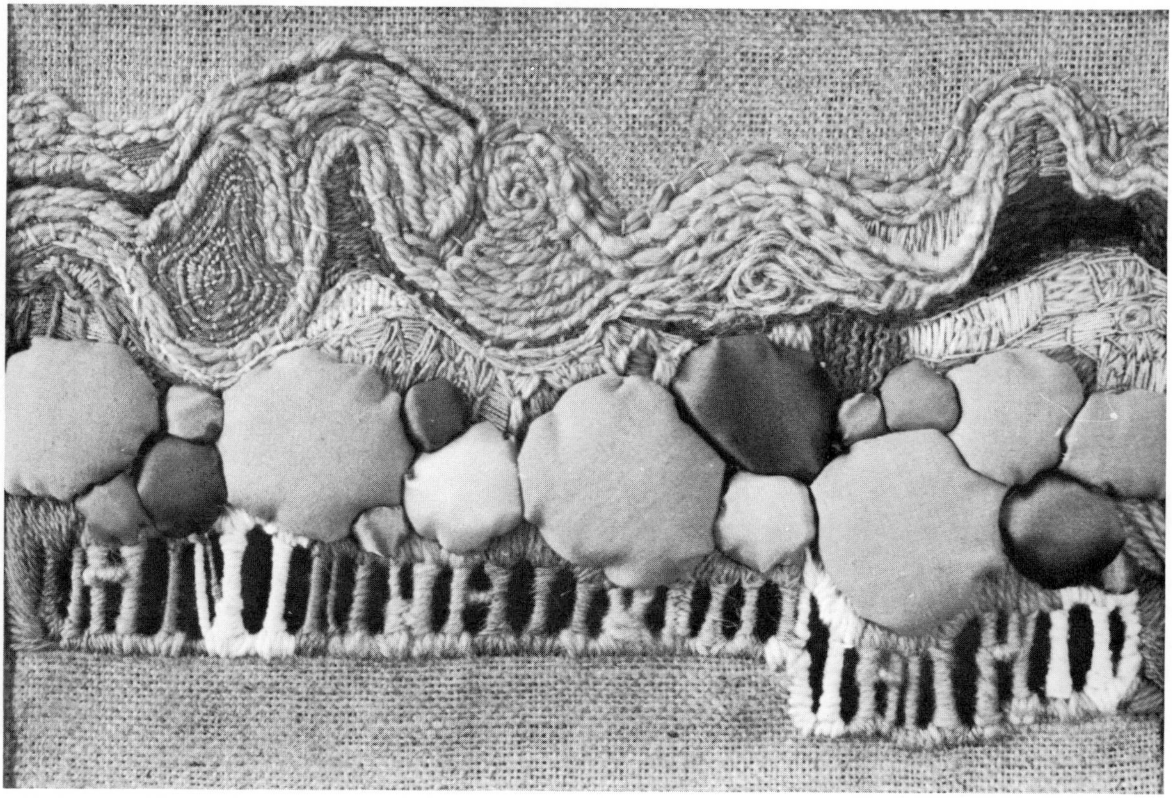

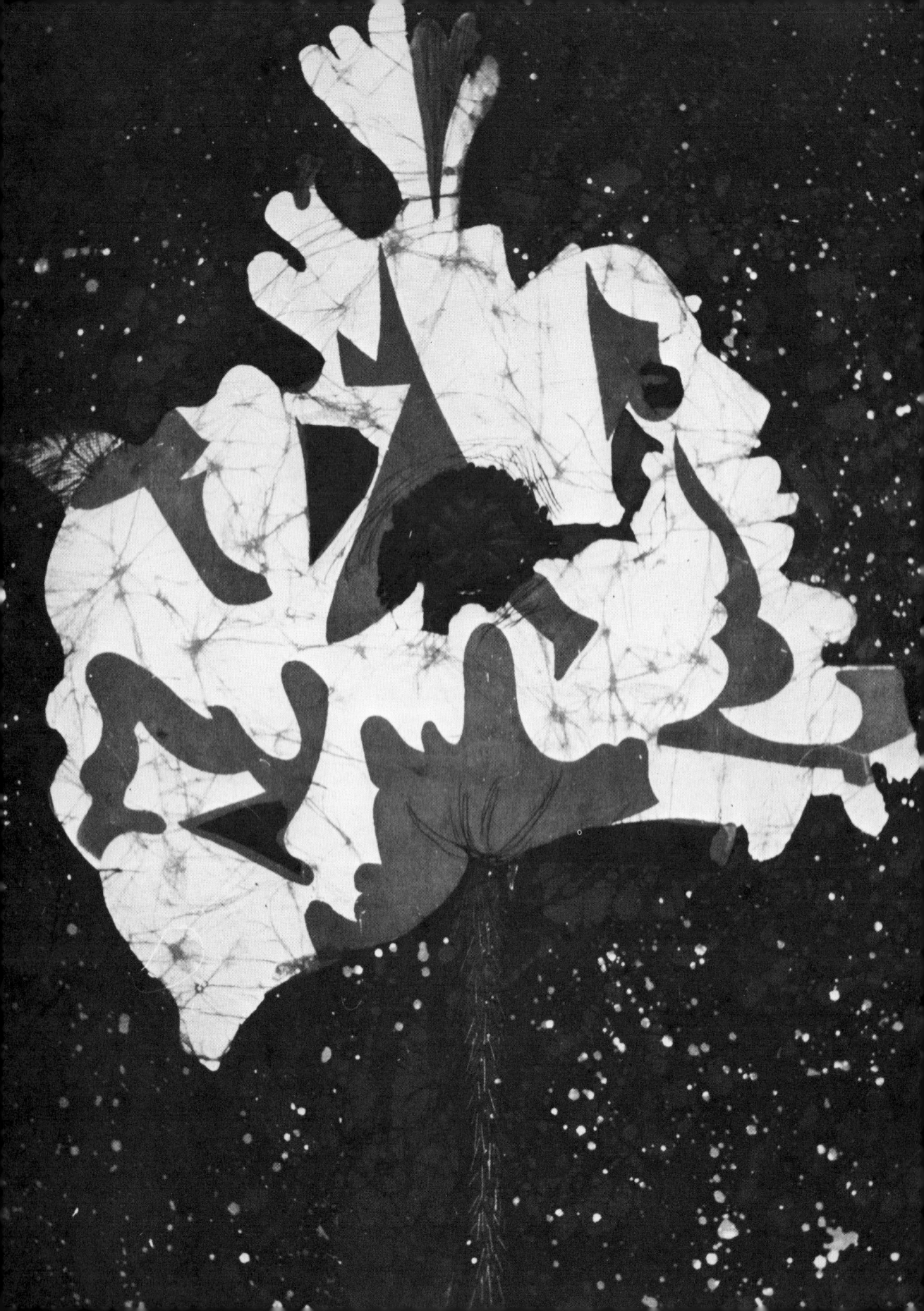

One of a series of photographs of the poppy were taken to reinforce the drawings in a sketchbook poppy

Poppy in the Sun by Carol Walklin
Careful planning was needed to select which media would best suit the characteristics to be described. To suggest the shining quality of the flowerhead amongst the dark foliage a batik background was made with red over green. Some of the red was allowed to 'marble' over the petal areas making a pink for the flower shape which was left mainly white. The cast shadow shapes were painted on Kodatrace and transferred photographically on to a screen, overprinting the lighter flowerhead with darker reddish 'shadows'. This technique retained the crispness of the original image
Finally the centre was heavily padded with a shiny green fabric, overlaid with dark threads and some bugles added. Some very fine stitchery was used to 'draw' the fine hairs on the bud, stem and leaf

Sketchbook studies showing the consideration of the selection of techniques which will provide the best rendering and interpretation of the subject

People

In English embroidery the human figure is often seen, and anyone interested in textiles is familiar with the small, exquisite figures decorating clerical garments like the fourteenth century *Syon Cope* (Victoria and Albert Museum, London). These are styalised figures, the techniques themselves influencing the nature of the forms, until the nineteenth century when excessive realism became popular. In the first half of the twentieth century, the human figure became more abstracted, sometimes sentimentalised but with the new machine techniques designers were able to 'draw' in a linear way, or build up areas swiftly and effectively, giving a different character to the image.

As drawing and painting directly on to the fabric background became accepted forms of media, the faces and figures were seen more often, but still in a lesser degree that natural form in the remaining sense. The drawing of the human figure has always been a tremendous challenge and seems to possess more pitfalls and strenuous disciplines than less testing subjects.

People can be seen singly or in a group – as pure portraiture or as something more symbolical. They can illustrate a story, ancient or contemporary, comment on society or our environment. People do not easily become transferred into the media of fabric and thread. It *can* be done with skill and humour as seen in the Bayeux Tapestry. Here, they record, amuse, decorate but are very formalised. Designers of today do present a blend of portraiture and comment and the picture on page 9 where the figure, by emphasis and distortion, demands our attention with his cry 'Al fuoco', appears hardly as flesh and blood, he is nevertheless immensely powerful and still, in essence, a *person* representing many people.

Left   *Detail of the* Bradford Table Carpet
Victoria and Albert Museum, London

Playground   *A photographic screenprint (photographic stencil) with the wire netting effect obtained by placing actual chicken wire with the drawing on film and exposing them simultaneously. Dark grey printing on a lighter grey sailcloth. Metal bars and some texturing made with machine embroidery, also some additional felt tip drawing Mary Newland*

Opposite *Sketch of Solzhenitsyn by Barbara Siedlecka*

*Portraits of
Solzhenitsyn
Jimmy Hendrix
A miner
by Barbara Siedlecka*

Origins *Small photographic heads in the press from which drawings were made, developing away from the vaguer, more tonal qualities of the reproductions towards a more linear approach. The lines emphasise the individual characteristics of the subject*
Media *The heads were painted in fabric dyes on to satin and then machine quilted, drawing directly on the fabric with a continuous line. Some parts have additional 'trapunto' padding, so raising parts of the design in varying heights – the lips, cheekbones and so on*
The area of the popstar's hair has been given extra texture by placing the satin over a coarse floor tile and making a rubbing, using a Fabricrayon.
Size *The heads are 33 cm (13 in.) square, mounted over Sundela board and have been set into 'trays' of plastic, 50 mm (2 in.) deep*
Photograph by Jan Siedlecki

56

Barbara Siedlecka
Birdbath   *The fascination of patterns and rhythms in disturbed water, the fragmentation of shapes and the partial views of form all show in these studies for the 'Birdbath'*
At first it appears as a linear exploration, going on to experimentation with painting with dyes, crayoning and machining, finally revolving into the image worked on jersey fabric
Quilting plays an important part in lifting the surface and reinforcing form and imagery. The whole figure is set in a vinyl, white padded 'bath' 150 cm × 60 cm
(5 ft × 2 ft) completing the scene are silver kid hot and cold taps
Photographs Jan Siedlecki

58

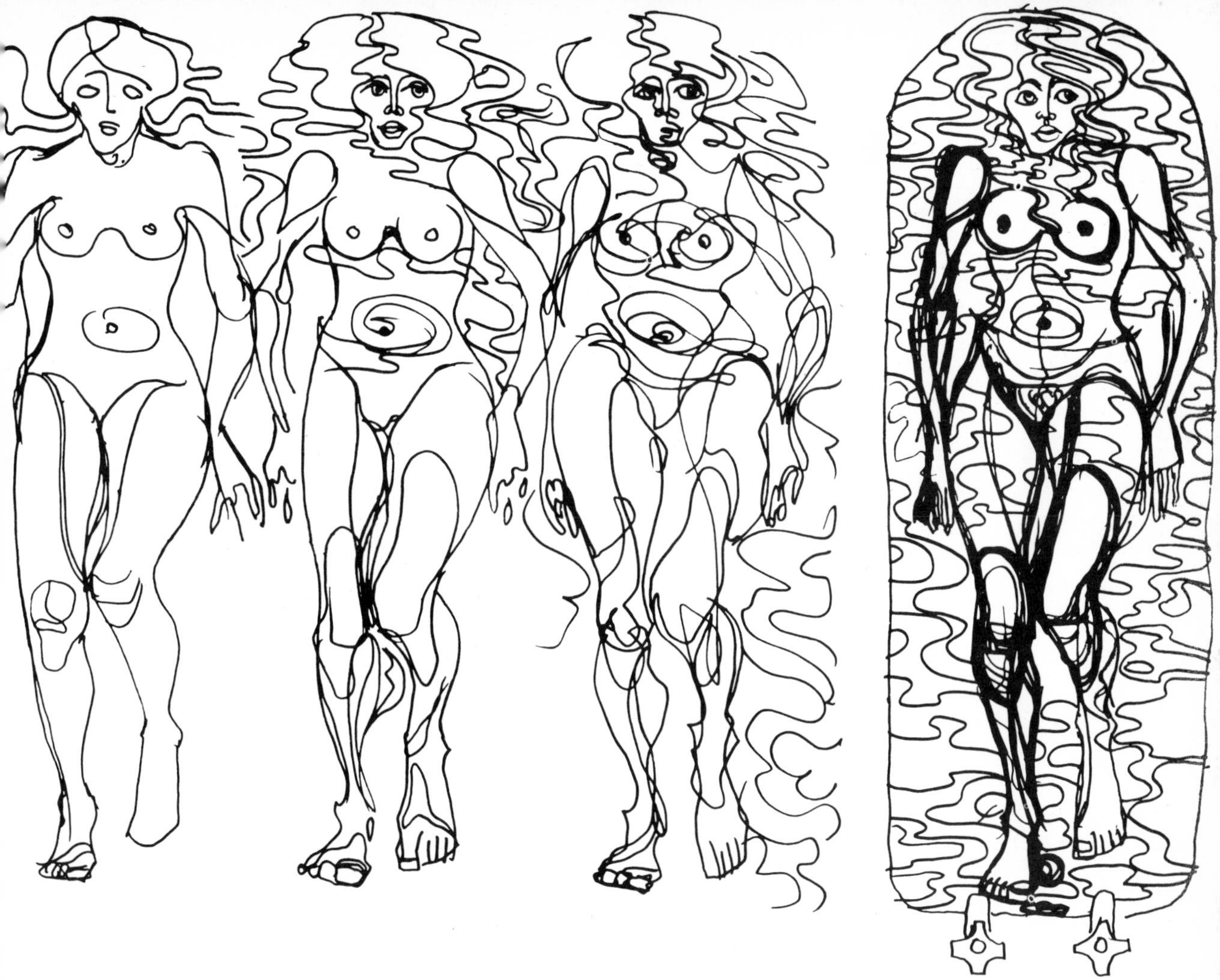

Exploits of Perseus *The screen has mostly been made with collage, hand and machine embroidery playing a lesser part. Preliminary drawings used as a means of discovery are essential at the outset, a necessary part of the planning. Before the actual fabrics are touched problems of space, tone, colour are resolved. A large template is made, all the pieces of material are applied first with glue and finally with the sewing machine. Intricate and essential details are completed with very simple hand stitching Richard Box*

The story of Perseus is narrated with the simplest of means but has great richness of colour and textures. These create a sumptuous final image   Richard Box

Graphics

The qualities related to 'graphics' in its widest sense are:

> problem-solving
> abstracted
> drawn
> symbolical
> linear
> structural
> optical
> mathematical
> depersonalised

There must be others but apart from actually designing for print in the purest interpretation of graphics the old connotations of 'commercial art' can be dismissed and much wider and deeper meanings be added in this field. Structural abstracted forms, significant colours, optics and mathematics, there are many new approaches open to the designer who wishes to work on fabric. 'Pop' art has made people more aware of the ordinary things around us and of the graphic qualities in many of these objects. *Letterforms* feature prominently, they too, are always with us in a literate society, or other symbols for the less literate. Lettering provides instant structures on which to build individual work, not always minding if the meaningful symbol is lost in controlled abstraction. The existing forms can provide a direct and absorbing basic 'geometry' from which new ideas can spring with contour, inter-spacing, structure, repetition.

Images on fabric can stem from the restrictions of simple grids. Although impersonal, they do make a starting point and unique work can develop from what are apparently cold and rigid beginnings. It is a reliable structure and discipline for the designer for a simple square divided many times and ways may offer an infinite number of solutions which may end as work of delicacy and charm, as the use of colour, tone, texture will alter and transfigure the original grid.

New energies are created, new forces brought into being as you make optical tensions, or show a disturbing balance of shape. This is a different kind of excitement from those mentioned in previous sections, but can still be an expression of an individual's sense of wonder which he wishes to share.

Above right   *Using the letter 'A' overlapped, to form a grid. The weight and grouping and direction of the lines create a optical effect*
Below right   *A screenprint (photographic stencil) in black on white fabric, based on a selected part of the drawn design (above). Trapunto quilting in some areas giving variety to the surface   Mary Newland*

Left *A large collage made of padded suede and leather with stainless steel rods Maureen Pickard*

Design based on a template of a lower case 'a' Mary Newland

Screenprint development from above

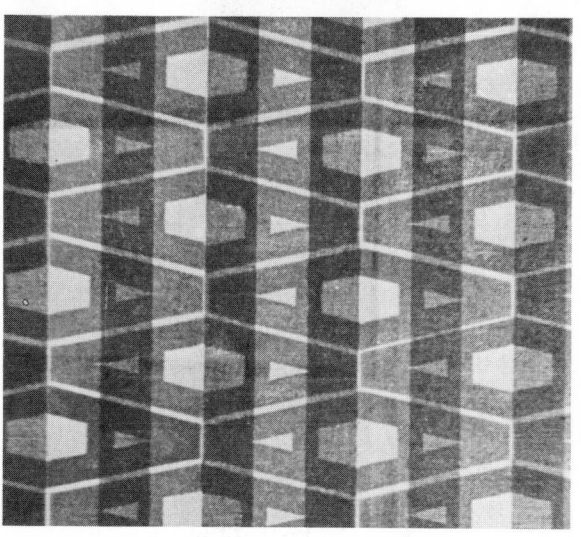

Woodblock 'A' printed as a repeat on a striped fabric background Margaret Livermore

Left *Plastic rings glued on to striped ticking. Interspaces have been filled with differing areas Lesley Lim*

Paper collage using newsprint and black paper to make a tonal image. Preparation for a fabric print Lesley Lim

Creative use of arranged letterforms to build up a whole image. Screenprinted on fabric in two colours Mary Newland

Collections

Collections fall into two main groups, public collections in museums and galleries and our own personal hoards.

Museum studies can be approached in many ways. One, is to go with an open, receptive, mind. This is a difficult approach as usually there is so much to see and stimulate us that we end up with a headache and not much that can be of use in our notebooks. Alternatively, we can go in search of a particular thing or theme. A time in civilisation perhaps, an ethnic group, a certain material, a technique and so on, *limiting* ones activity and concentration. A carefully selected motif may be studied and then translated into a personal interpretation, trying though, to keep its original qualities intact. At other times you may be looking for reinforcement of work already in hand or in the head – a prehistoric skeleton or a Romanesque sculptured figure.

Some far-sighted teachers encourage the collector's instinct in their pupils. They are never in short supply of stimulating and varied objects to draw, analyse, or paint. A stimulating environment affects us all, and a good early education in looking and selecting will continue to add richness to life, visually.

Our own collections can be acquired over a long period – things like old toys, stuffed birds and animals; china; dried flowers and grasses; shells, bones; buttons, machine parts – anything in fact. Markets and jumble sales provide starters for designs and ideas and also for the bits and pieces that are going to be needed to carry out these ideas. These are invaluable to the new-style embroiderer who now needs more than a neat work box and thimble, and whose necessities will probably include multipurpose glue and a saw!

Japanese armour, Victoria and Albert Museum, London

Worksheet of museum studies of Japanese armour where roundels and interlacing offer inspiration for interpretation in printing and embroidery   Mary Newland

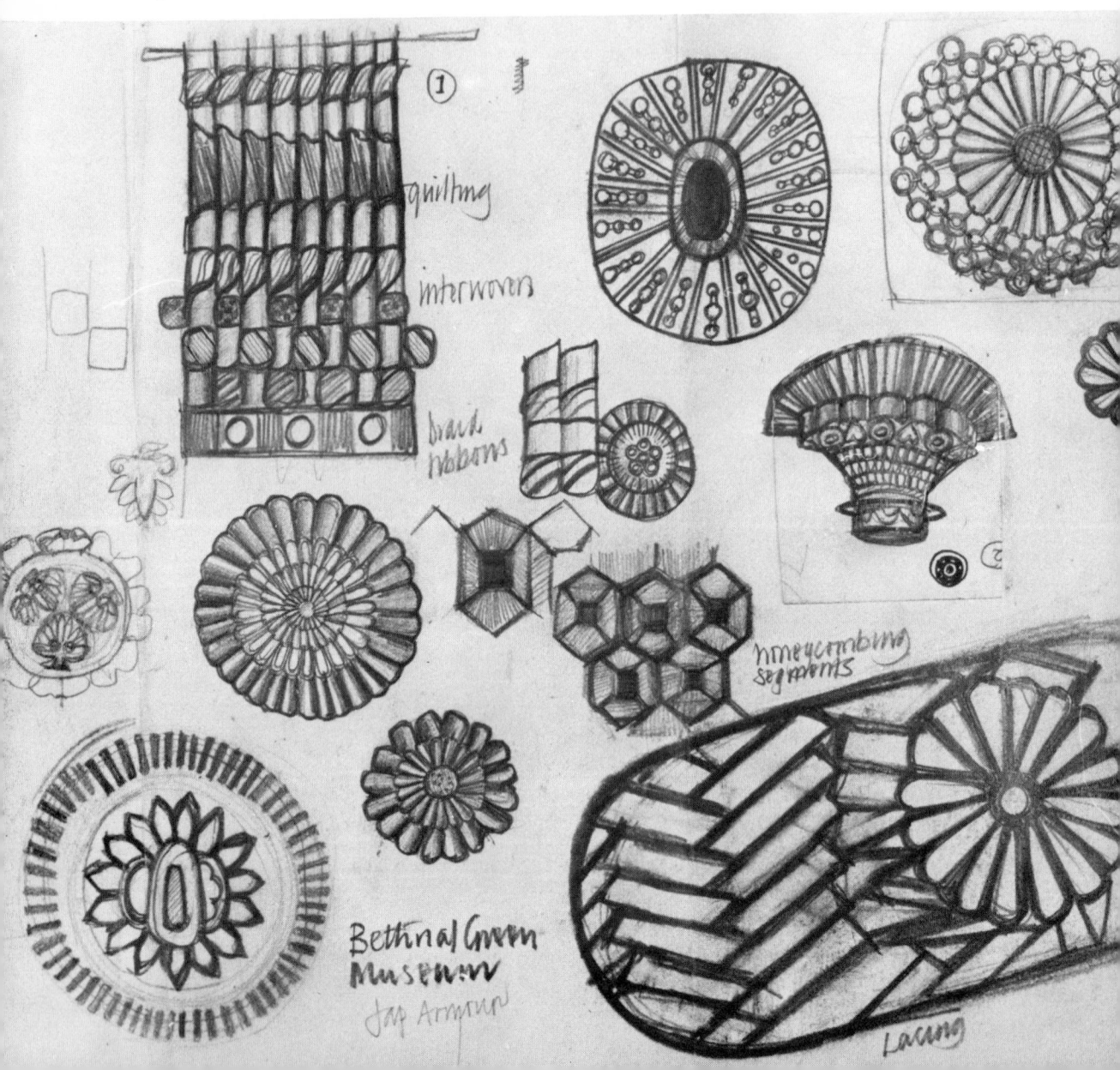

The sample below shows a small area of a fabric which has been quilted. Some parts are screenprinted and there is additional machine stitching based on part of the Japanese armour which had very strong, padded and interlaced qualities

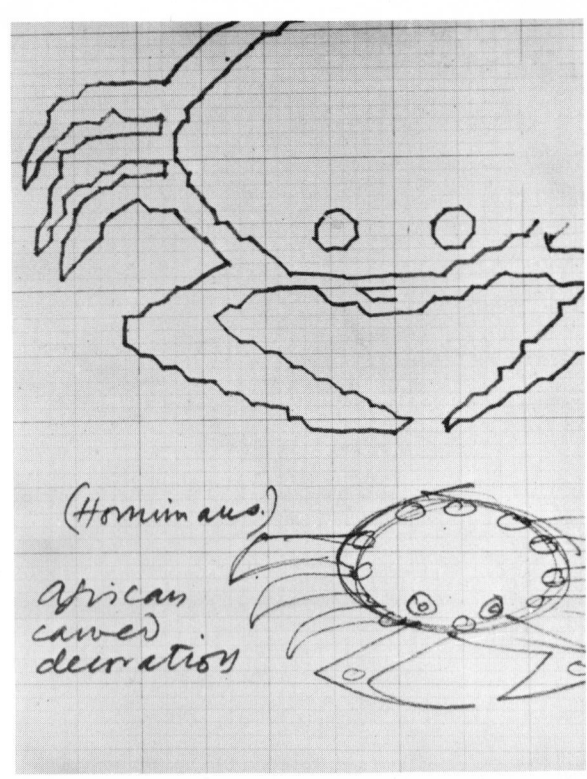

(Hominaus.)

African
carved
decoration

*Study of an African carved
decoration has been used as a motif
for a canvas work sampler in reds
and blacks   Carol Walklin*

Egyptian jewel *Embroidered interpretation of the jewel using some collage, laid threads, safety-pins, Lurex thread, and buttons covered with glued, spiralled silks (Unfinished) Yvonne Owen*

75

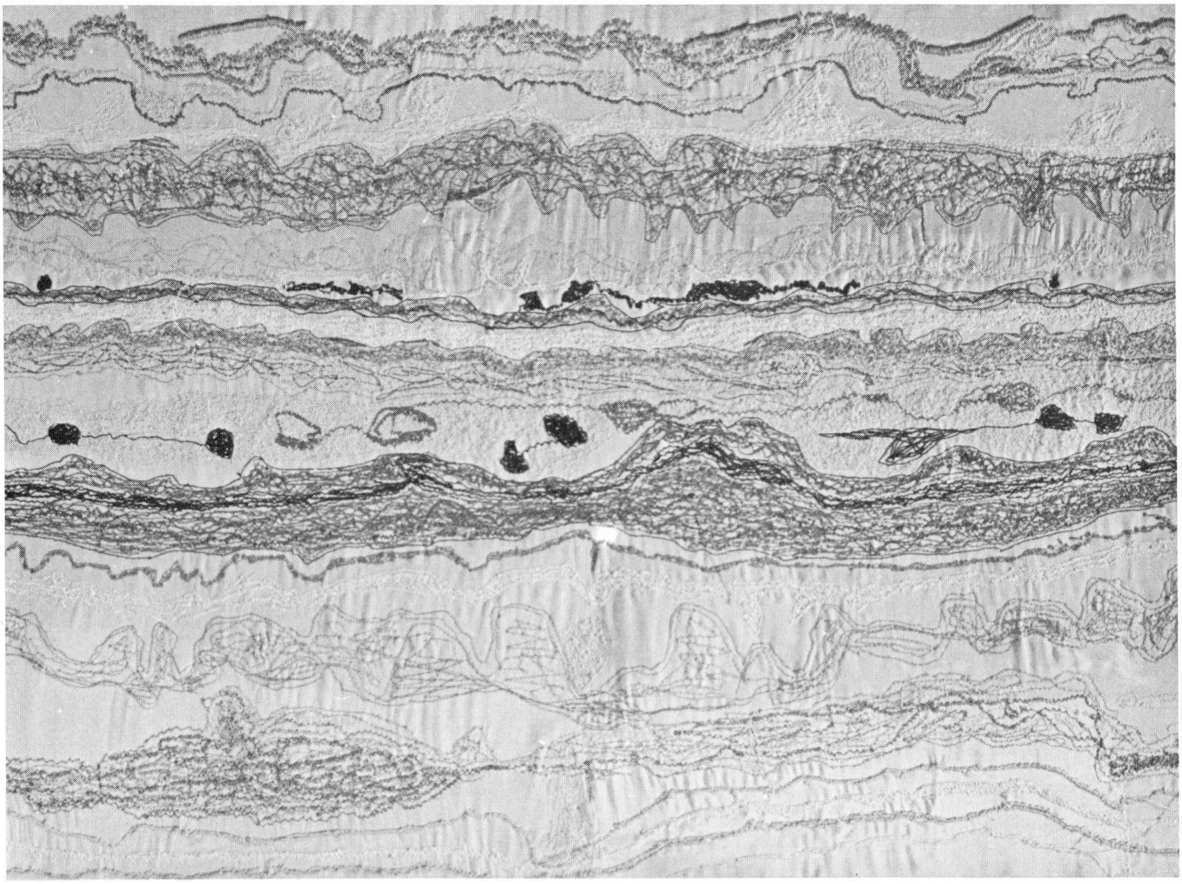

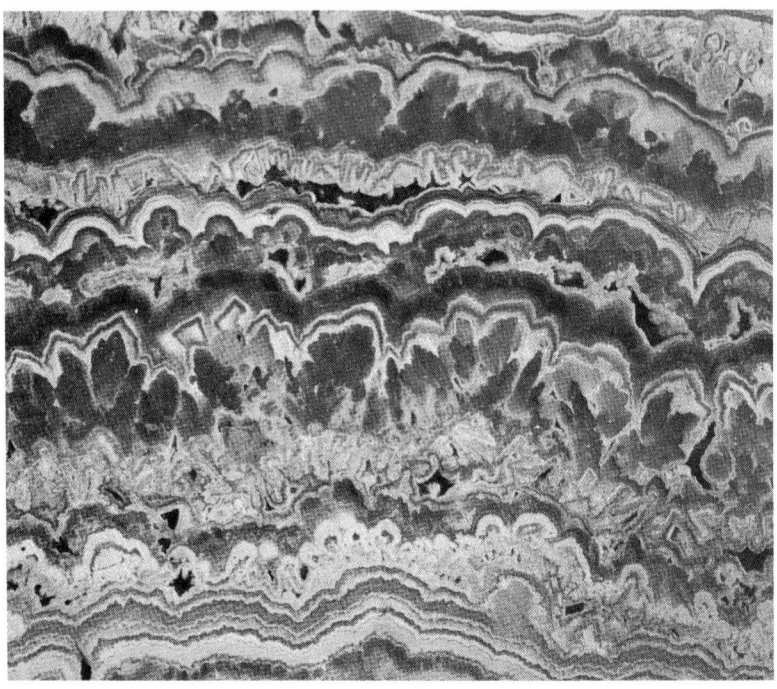

Example *Collaged areas of pink and ochre bands of coloured silky fabric, overstitched with rhythmical lines of darker tones of reds, umbers, yellows. Some clusters of stitches. (First exercise in machine embroidery)* Geraldene Festenstein

Polished slab of Rhodochrosite

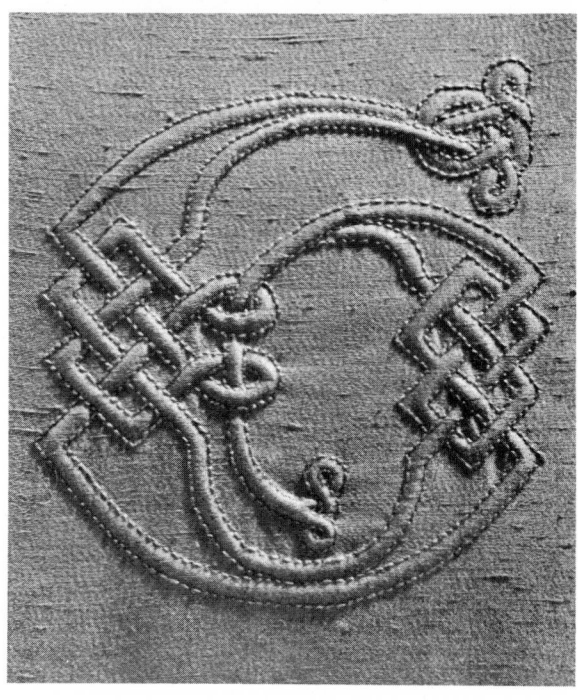

Example *Quilted 'C' reminiscent of a medieval initial. The corded quilting was done by hand in back stitch Eirian Short*

Slides can be made in hinged holders (used for colour photography). These are ideal for sections, or flat, small objects like a pillow feather. A certain amount of transparency is necessary in order to gain the full value of the selected objects when they are projected. Very high magnification can be stimulating, being beyond the scope of normal vision

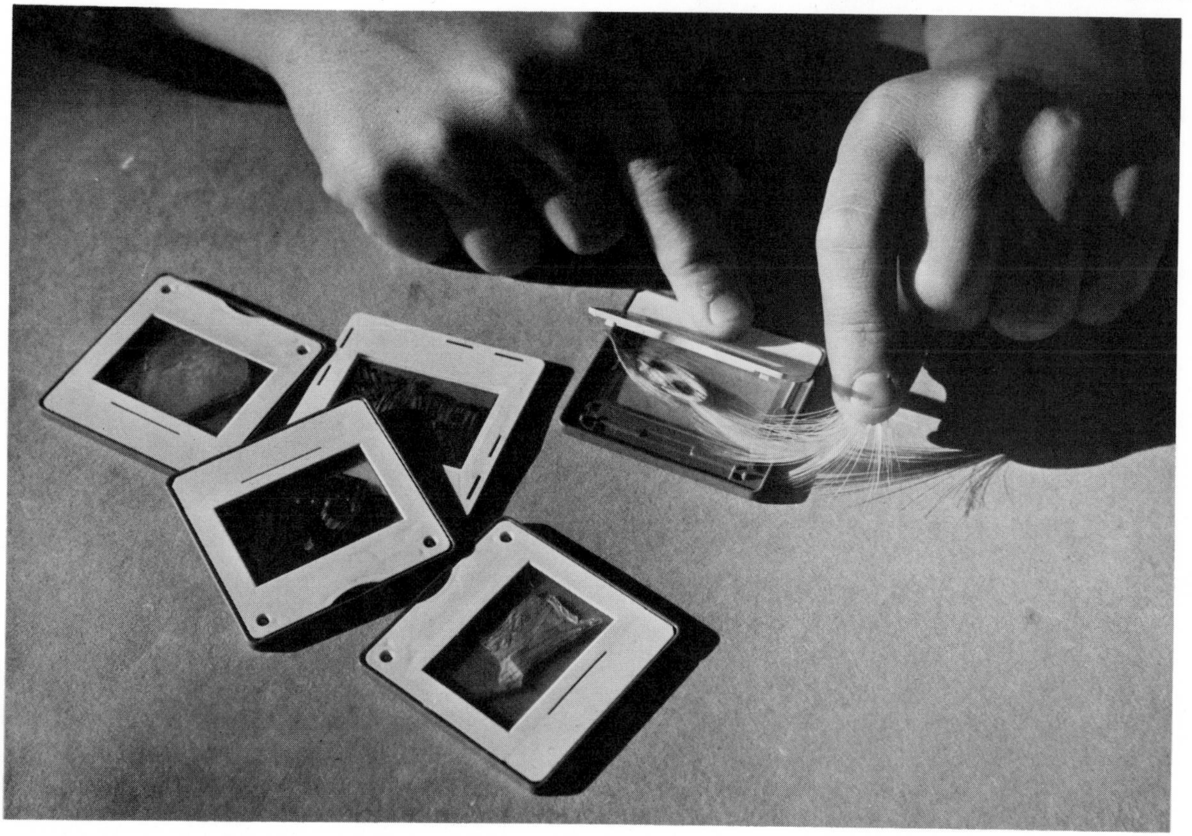

Japanese doll *The charm of the doll lies in her stillness but the twist of the body implies movement. Although the actual dress fabric is richly decorated the shapes are simplified for a screenprint (photographic stencil) image on a rich beige fabric background. Areas of white, dark blue and soft red suggested decoration and additional colour was used in the minimal stitchery, black thread for the emphasis of the hair, and a little light green and pink in knots and straight stitching on the robe itself*
Carol Walklin

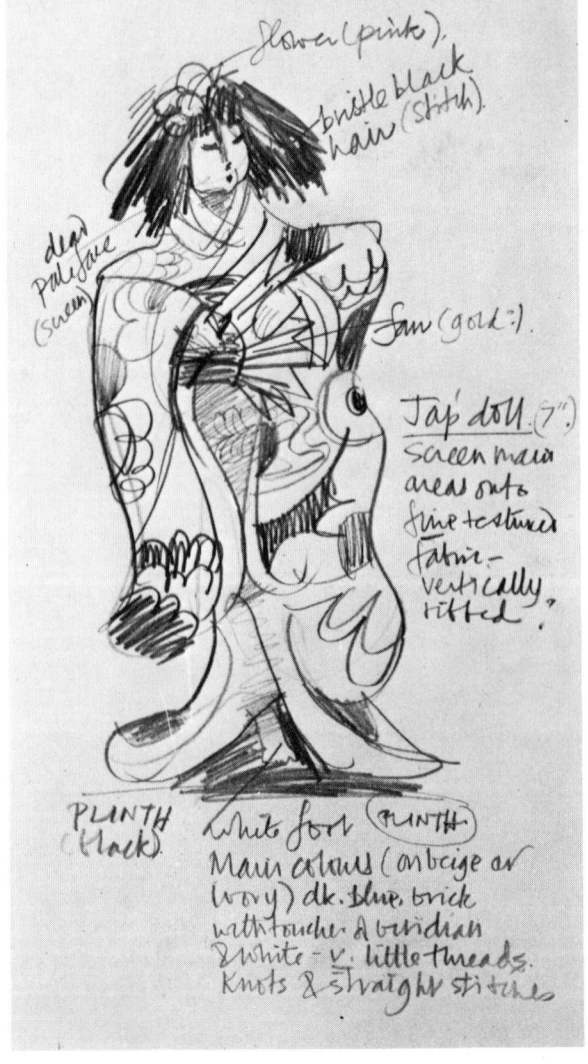

Looking forward

Opposite *Details, left to right:*
The Hero of a Hundred Fights *by Turner*
The Tate Gallery, London

Supernovae *by Vasarely*
The Tate Gallery, London

Le Pont de Courvevoie *by Seurat*
The Courtauld Institute of Art, London

The Cornfield *by Van Gogh*
Stedelijk Museum, Amsterdam

Looking again at the approaches, progressions and developments shown in this book, our original feelings are reinforced as to the essential values of sound, personal selection and the disciplines of drawing and design.

It sometimes seems that embroidery can escape all too easily from the high standards of fine art, becoming mere decoration. Such works show poor understanding of the real 'basics' that should be behind all good designing. (Obviously this remark excludes the use of decorative embroidery in its rightful place, much of which is both elegant and skilful.)

The emotions that trigger off a desire to do a piece of work sometimes become over-dominant, and although a feeling of response or excitement is necessary in the initial stages, it must eventually be harnessed by the disciplines of planning, drawing, selection and so on.

The present-day student is conscious of a media market which is ever changing, giving possibilities of using new techniques on fabric, and thereby increasing the scope of the designer. The rapidly rising cost of threads and fabrics encourages us to be more adventurous, and the solving of these mundane problems may well result in work that is both unique and exciting.

There is obviously always a need for expertise, good embroidery techniques, and all printers know the importance of doing their craft well and efficiently. But the emphasis in this decade is less on technical merit and more on the 'thinking' part of the design. This is not as intellectual as it sounds, as any enthusiast can follow a series of simple steps which become progressively easier with practise. The appropriate techniques will fall into their rightful places and instinct be reinforced with a sound knowledge of the skills to be used as a means of expression.

It is natural to suppose that embroiderers will visit exhibitions of textiles, and embroidery shows whenever possible, but it is important that they also go to other sources for inspiration such as museums, art galleries, photographic institutes, and libraries. They should not be looking for 'copybook' ideas but rather they should be searching for material of the highest visual standards. It is important to study the varied subjects and approaches of artists of repute, for often they describe so eloquently, with their extensive visual 'vocabulary', the elements of line, shape, colour, pattern and texture.

Van Gogh's drawings and painting with their tremendous linear qualities, relate to embroidery, his thick and thin strokes showing vigour and variety – the exciting and sensuous shapes of Matisse, deceptively simple – the contrasting approaches to colour in the pointillistic technique of Seurat, and the softer vibrations of light in the works of Turner – the interaction of colours and shape by Vasarely with his organised optical effects – the rich and decorative patterns of the medieval illuminated manuscripts – these 'descriptions', and many others, will serve to heighten our own awareness of these particular qualities, which are the basic elements of design so essential to all good embroidery.

Mary Newland
Carol Walklin 1977

83

Further reading

Fabric printing and dyeing
Introducing Batik, Evelyn Samuel, Batsford London:
  Watson-Guptill New York
Screen Printing on Fabric, Valerie Searle and Roberta
  Clayson, Studio Vista
Introducing Screen Printing, Anthony Kinsey, Batsford
  London: Watson-Guptill New York
Introducing Dyeing and Printing, Beryl Ash and Anthony
  Dyson, Batsford London: Watson-Guptill New York
Ideas for Fabric Printing and Dyeing, Peter Gooch, Batsford
  London: Watson-Guptill New York
Introducing Surface Printing, David Green, Batsford
Batik, Norma Jameson, Studio Vista
Screen Printing Techniques, Silvie Turner, Batsford London:
  Watson-Guptill New York
Dyes from Plants Seonaid Robertson, Van Nostrand
  Reinhold, New York
Fabric Printing and Dyeing, Peter Green, MacGibbon and
  Kee London
Fabric Printing Gisela Hein, Batsford London: Van
  Nostrand Reinhold New York

Stitches
100 Anchor Embroidery Stitches, J & P Coats Ltd, Glasgow
Simple Stitches, Anne Butler, Batsford London
Machine Stitches, Anne Butler, Batsford London

Embroidery
Inspiration for Embroidery, Constance Howard, Batsford
  London: Branford Newton Centre, Massachusetts
Embroidery and Colour, Constance Howard, Batsford
  London: Van Nostrand Reinhold New York
Pattern and Embroidery, Anne Butler and David Green,
  Batsford London: Branford Newton Centre,
  Massachusetts
Machine Embroidery, Christine Risley, Studio Vista
Machine Embroidery: Technique and Design, Jennifer Gray,
  Batsford London: Branford Newton Centre,
  Massachusetts
Metal Thread Embroidery, Barbara Dawson, Batsford
  London: Watson-Guptill New York

Fine Art and Design
Design as Art, Bruno Munari, Pelican
Painting, Peter Owen, Oxford University Press
Basic Design: The Dynamics of Visual Form, de Sausmarez,
  Studio Vista
Looking and Seeing Series, Kurt Rowland, Ginn
Learning to See, Kurt Rowland, Ginn
Creative Drawing – Point and Line, Ernst Röttger and
  Dieter Klante, Batsford
You can Draw, Kenneth Jameson, Studio Vista
Surfaces in Creative Design, Ernst Röttger, Dieter Klante
  and Friedrich Salzmann, Batsford
Approaches to Drawing, Leo Walmsley, Evans

Several of the titles mentioned here may well be out of print.
The technical information which they contain is, however,
valuable so it is worth while searching for them in libraries or
in second-hand shops.

Opposite   *Detail from panel
page 38 Joan Egan*

Suppliers

SUPPLIERS IN GREAT BRITAIN

Fabric printing dyes
E J Arnold Ltd (School Suppliers)
Butterley Street, Leeds LS10 1AX
(for Polyprint Dyes, minimum order value £5)
Berol Ltd, Oldmedow Road, Kings Lynn, Norfolk *(for Fabricol Dyes)*
Brico Commercial Chemical Company Ltd, 55–57 Glengall Road, London SE15 6NQ *(for Helizarin)*
Dylon International Ltd, Worsley Bridge Road, Lower Sydenham London SE26 5HD *(for Procion M Dyes and Dylon Cold Dyes)*
Nottingham Handcraft Company (School Suppliers), Melton Road West Bridgford, Nottingham NG2 6HD *(for Dytex Reeves Craft Dyes Polyprint and Dylon Cold Water Dyes)*
Polyprint Ltd, 815 Lisburn Road Belfast BT9 7GX *(for Polyprint Dyes)*
Reeves and Sons Ltd, Lincoln Road Enfield EN1 1SX, Middlesex *(for Reeves Craft Dyes)*
George Rowney and Co Ltd, 12 Percy Street, London W1A 2BP *(for Rowney Fabric Printing Dyes)*
Selectasine, Bulstrode Street, London W1 *(screen printing specialists)*
Sericol Group Ltd, 24 Parsons Green Lane, London SW6 4HS *(for Screen Printing Dyes and equipment)*
Winsor and Newton Ltd, Wealdstone HA3 5HR, Middlesex. London Showroom 51–52 Rathbone Place London W1P 1AB *(for Procion Dyes – sold in small quantities)*

Embroidery threads, fabrics and accessories
Mary Allen, Turnditch Derbyshire
E J Arnold Ltd (School Suppliers) Butterley Street, Leeds LS10 1AX
Art Needlework Industries Ltd, 7 St Michael's Mansions, Ship Street Oxford OX1 3DG
The Campden Needlecraft Centre High Street, Chippling Campden Gloucestershire
Craftsman's Mark Ltd, Broadlands Shortheath, Farnham, Surrey
Dryad (Reeves) Ltd, Northgates Leicester LE1 2QR
The Felt and Hessian Shop 34 Greville Street, London EC1
B Francis, 4 Glenworth Street London NW1
Fresew, 97 The Paddocks, Stevenage Hertfordshire SG2 9UQ
The Handworkers' Market, 8 Fish Hill Holt, Norfolk
Harrods Ltd, Knightsbridge London W1
Hobby Horse, 54 Montgomery Street Eaglesham, Glasgow
Levencrafts, 54 Church Square Guisborough, Cleveland
Mace and Nairn, 89 Crane Street Salisbury SP1 2PY, Wiltshire
MacCulloch and Wallis Ltd 25–26 Dering Street, London W1R 0BH
The Needlewoman Shop, 146–148 Regent Street, London W1R 6BA

Nottingham Handcraft Company (School Suppliers), Melton Road West Bridgford, Nottingham NG2 6HD
Christine Riley, 53 Barclay Street Stonehaven, Kincardineshire AB2 2AR
Russell and Chapple Ltd, 23 Monmouth Street, London WC2 *(hessian and scrim)*
The Silver Thimble, 33 Gay Street Bath
J Henry Smith Ltd, Park Road Calverton, Woodborough, nr Nottingham
Elizabeth Tracy, 45 High Street Haslemere, Surrey
Mrs Joan Trickett, 110 Marsden Road Burnley, Lancashire

SUPPLIERS IN THE USA

Fabric printing dyes
American Cyanamid Co, Dyes
Division, Wayne, New Jersey 07470
(for Alizarin/Helizarin)
School Products Co Inc, 312 East 23
Street, New York, NY 10010
*(distributors for Dylon International
Ltd)*
Pearl Paint Co, 308 Canal Street, New
York, NY 10013 *(distributors of
Rowney Fabric Dyes)*
Regents Products, 251 East Grand
Chicago, Illinois 60611 *(distributors of
Rowney Fabric Dyes)*
Silk Screen Supplies Inc, 32 Lafayette
Avenue, Brooklyn, New York, NY
11217 *(for Screen Printing Dyes and
equipment)*
Winsor and Newton Inc, 555 Winsor
Drive, Secaucus, New Jersey, 07094
(for Printex Fabric Printing Colors)

**Embroidery threads and
accessories**
Appleton Brothers of London, West
Main Road, Little Compton, Rhode
Island 02837
American Crewel Studio, Box 553
Westfield, New Jersey 07091
American Thread Corporation
90 Park Avenue, New York
Bucky King Embroideries Unlimited
Box 124c, King Bros, 3 Ranch
Buffalo Star Rkc, Sheriden, Wyoming
82801
Casa de las Tejedoras, 1618 East
Edinger, Santa Ana, California 92705
Colonial Textiles, 2604 Cranbrook
Ann Arbor, Michigan 48104
Craft Kaleidoscope, 6412 Ferguson
Street, Indianapolis 46220
Dharma Trading Company, 1952
University Avenue, Berkeley, California
94704
Folklorico Yarn Co, 522 Ramona
Street, Palo Alto 94301, California
The Golden Eye, Box 205, Chestnut
Hill, Massachusetts 02167
Heads and Tails, River Forest
Illinois 60305
Leonida Leatherdale, Embroidery
Studio, 90 East Gate, Winnipeg
Manitoba R3C 2C3, Canada
Lily Mills, Shelby, North Carolina
28150
The Needle's Point Studio, 7013
Duncraig Court, McLean, Virginia
22101
Sutton Yarns, 2054 Yonge Street
Toronto 315, Ontario, Canada
Threadbenders, 2260 Como Avenue
St Paul, Minnesota 55108

Acknowledgment

Our grateful thanks go to all those people who have co-operated so kindly with us in the preparation of this book.

We realise our debt to Colin Walklin who showed much patience and great skill in the production of most of the photographs.

We thank all colleagues and friends for the loan of their work and photographs. We also thank the following: Thelma M. Nye of Batsfords for her continuing enthusiasm and support; Charles Griffiths, The Dean and students at the Sidney School of Education, Polytechnic of Central London; Edna Kirk, Warden of the Needlecraft Centre for Teachers, Exton Street, London, SE1, Inner London Education Authority, who provided in-service students with courses and a climate in which we all could work experimentally; Malcolm Dakin at the Adult Arts Centre, Beckenham, Kent, for able and sensitive tutoring; also to all the tutors involved in the in-service Textile Course, Department of Education and Science, held at the Goldsmiths College of Art (1974). We also appreciate the ready assistance of staff at The Tate Gallery, London and at the Victoria and Albert Museum, London.

MN and CW 1977

Index

Abstract 8, 10, 23, 64
Applied fabric 22, 30
Armstrong, Sheila 49

Baj, Enrico 9
Banister, Phil 37
Batik 17, 18, 50
Beaney, Jan 28, 29
Box, Richard 60-3
Buildings 36

Calico 32
Canvas 6, 74
Collage 8, 21-2, 32-5, 37-9, 60, 66, 68, 69, 76
Collections 70
Colour 10, 34
Composition 44
Craftsmanship 6

Direct drawing 8, 20
Dyes 30, 46, 56
Drawing 6, 24-5, 46, 54
Davidson, Diane 49

Egan, Joan 38, 84
Environment 14

Felt tip, 20, 31, 54
Festenstein, Geraldine 76
Fine art 6
French knots, see *knots*

Garner, Margaret 42-3
Garwood, Christine 2
Graphics 64

Hand stitching 22, 32-3, 37, 60, 80-1
Holders, photographic 79

Images 6, 8, 10
Irish machine 2

Jeapes, Anita 37

Knots 20, 43, 46, 52
Kooraram, Josette 39

Letterforms 65-7
Lim 68-9
Line 10, 34
Linear approach 15
Livermore, Margaret 67
Locke, Cathy 14

Manmade 34
Machinery 40-1
Machine stitching 16-7, 23, 31-3, 37-9, 48-9, 54, 58, 60, 71, 76
Mathewson, Rita 48
Museums 70, 73-4

Natural forms 28-9
Natural wool 14
Needleweaving 49
Newland, Mary 15-7, 31-2, 40-1, 55, 65, 67, 69, 71, 73

Observation 15
Owen, Yvonne 75

Padding 2, 6, 31, 33, 49, 52, 56, 58, 66
Painting 8, 30, 37, 46, 54, 58
Pastels 46
Pattern 10
Pencil 14-5
People 54
Perception 34
Photography 44
Pickard, Maureen 66

Quilting 23, 56, 58, 71, 73-4, 77

Rapidograph 32

Scale 14
Screenprinting
  paper stencil 37
  photographic stencil 16, 18, 31, 42-3, 46, 52, 54, 80-1
Selection 10, 14
Seurat 83
Shape 10
Short, Eirian 77
Siedlecka, Barbara 24-5, 36, 56-9
Simplification 10
Stitchery 6; see also *machine* and *hand*
Stringer, Joy 22

Technology 6
Template 60
Texture 6, 10, 24
Threads 20-1, 30
Tufting 31
Turner 83

Van Gogh 83
Vasarely 83
Vilene 39
Visual vocabulary 6, 82

Walklin, Carol 18-23, 34-5, 46-7, 50-3, 74, 80-1
Walklin, Sarah 33
Whatmore, Pamela 10, 15, 26-7, 30
Woods, Marion 14